liß schreibe ich zu

getzeuig zu Lunden den 2. ap...

Anno 16 16

Bernhardt Wilhelm von Waßbach

James I of Great Britain

op sülcken karen word Het goe
London over Straet gebracht

Lot

Een Porterofte
Arbeyder van London

CONTENTS

THE AGE OF SHAKESPEARE

François Laroque

DISCOVERIES

HARRY N. ABRAMS, INC., PUBLISHERS

Shakespeare is universally regarded as a genius; his works are read and performed everywhere. Yet he started life as the son of a glove maker and was given only an average education. Always intensely curious about the world around him, Shakespeare would later rely on scenes remembered from his childhood, common country customs and superstitions, and fairs and other popular entertainments as raw material for his plays—just as much as he would tales of kings and noblemen.

CHAPTER I
STRATFORD-UPON-AVON

The theater was a popular form of entertainment in the 16th century, as seen in this painting of a village fair (left) by Dutch artist David Vinckboons. Strolling players (right) toured through small towns.

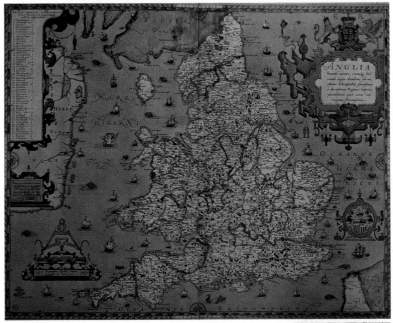

It was in about 1550 that a man named John
Shakespeare moved to Stratford-upon-Avon, in
central England. He came from the nearby
village of Snitterfield, where his father, Richard
Shakespeare, was a prosperous farmer. In Stratford
John Shakespeare started a glove-making business
and also traded profitably in wool and meat. In
1557 he married Mary Arden, the youngest of
Robert Arden's eight daughters; this wealthy family
lived in Wilmcote, a little hamlet near Snitterfield,
in the county of Warwickshire.

Stratford was a tranquil market town that lay in a
lovely wooded valley and was famous for its fairs.
London was two days away on horseback, four days
on foot, and the great Midland towns—Worcester,
Warwick, and Oxford—were within striking distance.

Stratford's strategic position at a crossroads on the
Avon River is suggested by the etymology of its name,

Stratford is at the heart
of England, as can be
seen on this 1579 map.
"This royal throne of
kings, this scepter'd isle, /
This earth of majesty, this
seat of Mars, / This other
Eden, demi-paradise"
(*Richard II,* II, i).

which means a "ford by which a Roman road crossed the river." Property of the bishops of Worcester in the Middle Ages, by the end of the 12th century the town had acquired a degree of autonomy. Two fine

churches of 13th-century origin survive today: the parish church of the Holy Trinity and the Guild Chapel. The Guild also built the grammar school, which was formally reestablished by Edward VI in the 16th century as the King's New School. Also in Stratford is the handsome stone bridge first constructed in 1490 by Sir Hugh Clopton, a local luminary who made his fortune in London and built New Place, a mansion there later bought by William Shakespeare.

John Shakespeare prospered in Stratford. In 1556 he bought two houses, one of them on Henley Street, where he had been lodging since 1552. Soon afterward he

John Shakespeare's business premises were in the west wing of his house on Henley Street, which, as far back as one can trace, was known as the "woolshop"—evidence that he traded in wool, and possibly skins, in addition to working as a glover. This contemporary engraving shows a craftsman making gloves and leather purses. True to his origins, Shakespeare did not forget the traditions of the craft in his plays, in which he made frequent use of glove imagery. The clown Feste in *Twelfth Night*, for example, gives this definition of wit: "A sentence is but a chev'ril glove to a good wit. How quickly the wrong side may be turn'd outward" (III, i).

entered public life, joining the town council in 1557, becoming an alderman in 1565 and a bailiff in 1568. The following year he unsuccessfully applied for a grant of a

A few words and a date recording Shakespeare's baptism: the first evidence we have of his existence.

coat of arms and, thereby, the right to be called a "gentleman." And here his social ascent was brought to an abrupt end. In 1577, burdened by heavy fines and increasing debt, he was obliged to mortgage his wife's property. For reasons that remain mysterious he ceased to attend the meetings of the council, which finally expelled him in 1586. He also stopped going to church, no doubt out of fear of running into his creditors.

Early Years

Opposite the date 26 April 1564 the Stratford parish register records the baptism of "Gulielmus filius Johannes Shakspere" ("William, son of John Shakespeare"). Born in a little house on Henley Street, William was the first son of John and Mary Shakespeare, the third of their eight children. Although the exact date of William's birth is not known, his birthday is celebrated on 23 April.

William attended a local school in Stratford. Starting at the age of four or five, children in the 16th century were taught to read, write, and count by a schoolmaster known as an "abecedarius."

The naive lack of proportion apparent in this engraving of an Elizabethan school suggests the awe in which the formidable "abecedarius" was held.

recited the alphabet using a hornbook and practiced their reading using the Bible. The children were introduced to Latin and were required to learn Latin maxims by heart. In his plays Shakespeare often presents schoolmasters in a somewhat ridiculous light, as for example the pedantic Holofernes in *Love's Labour's Lost* or the parson Sir Hugh Evans, who gives a memorable and obscene Latin lesson in *The Merry Wives of Windsor* (IV, i). Shakespeare also harks back to his school days in *As You Like It* (II, vii), with Jaques' speech on the seven ages of man: "the whining schoolboy, with his satchel / And shining morning face, creeping like snail / Unwillingly to school." The school day was long, from six o'clock in the morning to five in the afternoon, interrupted only briefly for a meal and a quick recess.

Later, at secondary school, which William would have entered at the age of eleven, pupils had to grapple with grammar, logic, and rhetoric. They

Shakespeare makes fun of schoolmasters in his comedies, as can be seen in this extract from the absurd Latin lesson given by Sir Hugh Evans to the boy William Page.

"EVANS: What is 'lapis,' William?
WILLIAM: A stone.
EVANS: And what is 'a stone,' William?
WILLIAM: A pebble.
EVANS: No, it is 'lapis,' I pray you remember in your prain" (*The Merry Wives of Windsor*, IV, i).

The figures on the title page of this Latin primer of 1607 symbolize the seven liberal arts.

continued their Latin studies, reading ancient Roman classics such as Ovid's *Metamorphoses* and *Heroides,* Virgil's *Aeneid,* and the works of Cicero, Horace, and Sallust. The students also learned Greek, starting perhaps with Lucian's *Dialogues,* written in the 2nd century AD, or exercises in translating the New Testament.

Shakespeare's schooling came to an abrupt end. Unlike his playwright contemporaries in London, the "university wits," he did not go to a university. This was an age in which a good secondary school pupil endowed with a strong sense of curiosity could become thoroughly self-educated. The fact that Shakespeare lacked higher education and social advantages proved no obstacle. His love of language and innate mastery of the art of the theater—combined with a tremendous capacity for work and fertile powers of invention—were enough to enable him to produce work of astonishing range.

The Rural World, the Seasons, the Cycle of Life

A descendant of farming stock, Shakespeare was steeped in rural tradition, and there is frequent reference in his works to nature—both flora and fauna. Plants and flowers are used with powerful symbolic effect in the queen's famous speech about Ophelia's death in *Hamlet* (IV, vii), following the scene in which the girl, stricken by madness, hands out flowers and herbs. In plays such as *Romeo and Juliet, A Midsummer Night's*

The herbals of the period included illustrations of herbs and flowers (left and right). Plant and animal life inspired much art, including the embroidered hunting scene and animal engravings below. Nature imagery is used frequently in Shakespeare's works.

"HOSTESS: I am no thing to thank God on ... thou art a knave to call me so.

FALSTAFF: Setting thy womanhood aside, thou art a beast to say otherwise.

HOSTESS: Say, what beast, thou knave, thou?

FALSTAFF: What

Dream, Othello, and *The Winter's Tale* (and also in the sonnets), roses, herbs, and autumn leaves are used to evoke the cycle of the seasons and mark the inexorable passage of time.

The animal world is also well

beast? Why, an otter.

PRINCE: An otter, Sir John! Why an otter?

FALSTAFF: Why, she's neither fish nor flesh: a man knows not where to have her."

Henry IV, Part 1 (III, iii)

represented in Shakespeare. Birds abound, especially the lark, messenger of day, and the nightingale, who sings at night. *Macbeth* is characterized by a preponderance of images of nocturnal birds and birds of prey—owls, kites, rooks, vultures, falcons, and crows. The Shakespearean bestiary includes bats, serpents, hedgehogs, and insects; insects appear figuratively as the fairy creatures in *A Midsummer Night's Dream* or in the Queen Mab speech in *Romeo and Juliet.* The bestiary also draws on the hunt, including references to a variety of game— hares, wild boar, and deer—with packs of dogs hot on their heels. In *As You Like It* the sight of a mortally wounded deer inspires an outpouring from Jaques, the moralist of the play.

Shakespeare goes beyond simple country wildlife, however, to include more exotic species, both foreign and imaginary. He mentions the rhinoceros, tiger, elephant, and bear, as well as the mythical unicorn, phoenix, and dragon. There were also heraldic animals, those creatures incorporated in the armorial bearings of the nobility: The bear, for

" You spotted snakes with double tongue, / Thorny hedgehogs, be not seen; / Newts and blind-worms, do no wrong, / Come not near our fairy Queen.**"**
A Midsummer Night's Dream (II, ii)

Trembling to see the ghost of Banquo—whose murder he had ordered—appear at a banquet for his subjects, Macbeth challenges the specter to assume a form he dare confront, such as that of "the armed rhinoceros" (*Macbeth,* III, iv), illustrated in this contemporary engraving.

example, was the emblem of the Warwicks, and the wild boar that of the Yorks.

Traditional bestiaries laid down an animal hierarchy. The lion, eagle, and dolphin symbolized divine kingship, whereas the donkey, pig, goat, rat, and monkey were impure animals, emblems of lechery. Because of the influence of theologians who specialized in demonology and the misogynist climate of the Middle Ages, serpents often represented women. This link was based not only on the seduction of Eve by the serpent in Genesis but also on the then popular system of physiology, which defined both female and snake as cold and moist.

Curiously, the hierarchy established in the animal world was reflected in people's culinary

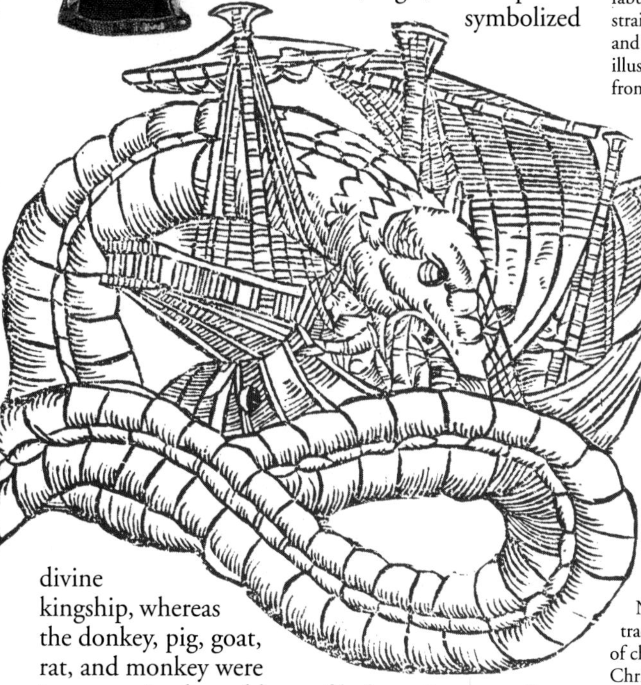

Over 3000 references to some 180 different species of animals—both real and imaginary—have been identified in Shakespeare's plays. His fabulous creatures came straight out of bestiaries and legends. Those illustrated here are taken from Edward Topsell's treatises *The History of the Serpents* (1608) and *History of Four-Footed Beasts* (1607). Sea serpents (left) seemed an ever-present danger to Elizabethan seafarers. The Hydra (below) figures as a symbol of the multitude in *Coriolanus*. The unicorn in the 16th-century tapestry (top left) from Oxburgh, Norfolk, was a traditional image of chastity and Christ's sacrifice.

habits, underlying, for example, the rules people observed during Lent, when they gave up meat and ate fish in its place—whether trout, eels, or oysters. Associations were made between man and meat, woman and fish. Similar eating patterns were designed to follow the movements of the signs of the zodiac and the planets, which were believed to regulate people's tempers and govern various parts of the human body. Shakespeare breathed new life into these beliefs by making them part of his characters' daily lives and incorporating them into the symbolism, attitudes, and folklore presented in his plays.

The images drawn from nature work as a whole to enrich dramatic argument and increase the plays' realism, which is born of the accumulation of concrete detail. In effect, Shakespeare's theater holds up a mirror to the world, reflecting its motley profusion in miniature.

Shakespeare clearly never abandoned popular culture, the world of oral tradition, legend, and ballad. His rustic scenes are often extraordinarily true to life, as in the dialogue of the carriers in *Henry IV,*

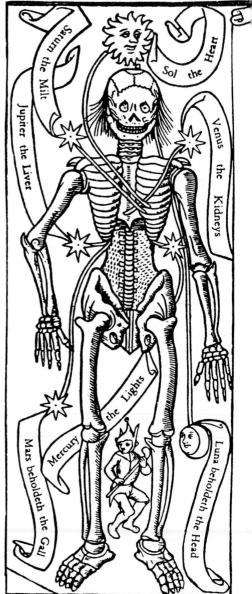

fama:

L ife in Shakespeare's day was anchored in tradition. The two period illustrations on this page can be seen as symbolic of the social structure: The queen (left), in all her pomp, pays a visit to the country, while a simple peasant woman (below) takes her geese to market.

Part 1 (II, i) before Falstaff and his men attack the pilgrims at Gadshill, or in the sheepshearing feast in *The Winter's Tale* (IV, iv). His recollections of fairs and markets and of dealers examining livestock or arguing over the price of wool frequently enliven his plays and give them both vitality and realism.

This engraving (opposite) by Guy Marchant, from *Kalendar and Compost of Shepherds* (1493), illustrates the influence of the planets on different parts of the body. The figure of a fool between the skeleton's legs is a reference to 15th-century morality plays.

A Visit from Queen Elizabeth I (1533–1603)

The popular celebrations and rituals that accompanied holidays and feast days in the countryside were an opportunity for the young Shakespeare to enjoy the performances of strolling players. Thanks to its position at a crossroads, Stratford was often visited by well-known troupes: that of the earl of Leicester in 1573 and 1576, of Lord Strange in 1579, of the earl of Essex in 1584, and the Queen's Men in 1587.

A visit by the queen herself, however, was a different matter. In July 1575 Elizabeth I came to Kenilworth Castle, near Stratford, to attend

the festivities planned in her honor by the earl of Leicester. The revelry, as lavish as it was brilliant, went on for three weeks in the presence of the queen's court. Open-air events were organized for the local people, who came from the surrounding countryside to greet their sovereign. Each day, each evening, brought some cleverly planned amusement, a mythological play or fireworks, all in the finest tradition of a Renaissance festival. These shows near his hometown must have given Shakespeare many opportunities to immerse himself in theater and develop an understanding of its magical effects.

Morris dancers near the Thames at Richmond (above).

Popular Theater, Processions, and Mysteries

During the Protestant Reformation religious holidays and feast days were reduced in number and greatly simplified. Puritans objected to the old holidays rooted in rural custom and based on the cycle of the seasons: The celebration of May Day, with its

maypole and traditional morris dancing, was openly attacked as a licentious revival of paganism and a manifestation of

In 1591 Elizabeth I visited the earl of Hertford, who held a display of water sports in her honor. A pond was specially dug in the shape of a crescent moon to evoke Diana, the goddess with whom the queen liked to be associated. This engraving (left) shows the queen, surrounded by her court, watching the spectacle. The engravings of musicians are from the 16th century.

devil worship. In *The Anatomie of Abuses*, published in 1583, the Puritan pamphleteer Philip Stubbes declared these ancient spring celebrations to be devilish rites. The may blossoms customarily used to adorn town squares and streets were torn down by aggrieved and zealous ministers. Villagers guilty of cutting trees and branches in the royal forests were punished with fines.

Ancient fertility rites lived on in popular memory nonetheless, and it was in popular culture that Shakespeare's theater had its roots. Old traditions survived in the form of mummers' plays, put on at Christmas and Easter, in the course of which valiant St. George, killed in combat with a giant or a Turkish knight, came back to life—thanks to a bottle of magic elixir—to triumph over his enemy.

The sacrificial aspect of the death and resurrection of the hero, enacted in the context of semipagan festivities, is also found in the mystery plays of the Middle Ages, in which scenes from the Old and New Testaments were acted out on traveling stages. These performances were held on Corpus Christi. Instituted in 1264 by Pope

The Puritans wrote fiery pamphlets denouncing pagan holidays such as May Day, with its maypole dance, illustrated here in Charles I's time. The hobbyhorse (top left), Robin Hood, Maid Marian, and the fool are the four chief dancers in a traditional morris dance.

The painting of the Last Judgment in the Guild Chapel at Stratford shows devils pushing the damned into Hell. During the Reformation it was pronounced unedifying

to the faithful and was whitewashed. (The watercolor opposite was rendered from what survived in 1807.)

Winter was the season of banquets and indoor entertainments. These early 17th-century watercolors of tavern scenes show a meal (left) and cardplaying (opposite). At Christmas actors and fools would put on impromptu performances in the houses of the nobility —a piece of improvised theater, perhaps, or a morning concert. The masqueraders arriving in this watercolor (right) recall the opening scenes of *Romeo and Juliet,* when Romeo and Mercutio and their friends disguise themselves and go to the ball given by Capulet: "This night I hold an old accustom'd feast, / Whereto I have invited many a guest, / Such as I love…. / At my poor house look to behold this night / Earth-treading stars that make dark heaven light…. *Enter Romeo, Mercutio, Benvolio, with five or six other Maskers…*" (I, ii–iv).

Urban IV, this is the last movable holy day in the Catholic calendar, falling between 21 May and 24 June. The time of year meant that the often lengthy plays could be acted in their entirety during daylight hours.

In addition to grandiloquent declamations by characters such as Herod—Hamlet refers to an actor who "out-Herods Herod" (III, ii)—the mystery plays featured boisterous squabbles between Noah and his wife and bawdy humor accompanying the entrance of the devils. By the 15th century morality plays became more secular in their handling of religious themes, introducing allegorical figures such as Everyman, Charity, Folly, and Pleasure. Plays such as *The Castle of Perseverance* were performed by strolling players in stately homes and town halls or on stages similar in construction to the big-top circuses of today.

Closely related to the morality plays were the interludes, short dramas that were performed between the courses of a banquet. They frequently took the form of long debates on the subject of marriage, punctuated by often obscene or scatological comic scenes acted by clowns known as "vices."

The flamboyant civic spectacles put on in the streets of medieval London and lasting for several days had their origin in pre-Reformation, religiously inspired "pageants." They were held on 23 April, St. George's Day; 24 June, St. John's Day; and 29 October, the day of the lord mayor's procession. In a series of often eccentric live tableaux, real and fabulous animals (dromedaries, unicorns, dragons) would pull carts on which actors or groups of children dressed as angels performed. The figures who led the processions were typically disguised as savages, bearing torches or firebrands to clear a passage through the crowd. In London all these spectacles were first organized by the guilds, for whom they were an occasion to display wealth and power. Later the shows were entrusted to dramatists. The spectacle in this painting (details below) of 1615, by Denis van Asloot, celebrated the Infanta Isabella's entrance into Brussels. (Isabella, 1566–1633, was married to Albert, the governor of the Spanish Netherlands.)

The Rich Memories of Sir Henry Unton

This anonymous painting, dated 1596, celebrates the life and death of diplomat Sir Henry Unton. The scene second from the right (detail below) shows a masque taking place in Unton's house. A procession advances in a spiral—three groups of ladies ascend the steps in pairs, hunters' bows and flowers in their hands, red masks over their faces. In the center is a small group of musicians. Above them a winged Mercury stands by the goddess Diana, who wears her traditional moon headdress and carries a bow and arrow. Ten cupids—five black and five white, an allegory of night and day—carry torches, casting a mysterious light over the scene. The rest of the painting depicts Unton's birth, career, funeral, and tomb.

Rites of Passage: Baptism, Marriage, and Funeral

Little written evidence of Shakespeare's life survives beyond the dates of his baptism and marriage, duly inscribed in the parish register. Even so, we know that the stages of a person's life were customarily marked by rites of passage valued both as traditions and for their religious significance. These rites, dating back to the Middle Ages, were portrayed in allegorical form in a good number of paintings and engravings, one example of which is the painting of the birth, life, and death of Sir Henry Unton (pp. 32–3). Shakespeare, too, makes reference to the several stages of a person's life—most familiarly in *As You Like It*.

Notwithstanding the Reformation, the rites accompanying these various ceremonies had been preserved for an important reason. They were considered necessary to ward off evil spirits and guard against the wicked doings of fairies, who could—if not properly managed—substitute a misshapen child, or a changeling, for an infant in its cradle. Nuptial festivities for the nobility often included a masque, or dramatic entertainment, featuring Hymen (the Roman goddess of marriage) or Juno (the Greek goddess of marriage); music and dance added to the gaiety of the occasion. Full funeral rites were also believed essential to the repose of the soul of the deceased. However, the financial crisis affecting the aristocracy in the late 16th century—the result of the breakdown of the manorial and feudal systems—led to a reduction in the ostentatiousness with which such events were celebrated.

Fairies, Witches, and Other Wonders

Goblins, fairies, and sprites, such as Puck, also known as Robin Goodfellow, were not particularly well regarded in the popular belief of the time. They were disturbing little creatures who appeared only at night and played tricks on people, pinching them, driving them mad, luring them into their underground kingdoms, or terrifying them with nightmares.

Shakespeare created an important role for these creatures from Celtic folklore that had been made fashionable by the pageants staged for the queen on her visits to the country. In *A Midsummer Night's Dream* fairy king Oberon and queen Titania are human in size, nocturnal doubles, as it were, of the characters Duke Theseus and the Amazon Hippolyta. Shakespeare tends to play down the malevolent nature of

From birth to death, cradle to coffin, and finally as a skeleton, a person's life was divided into the seven ages portrayed in this anonymous 16th-century painting (below left). Marriage was a major event and an occasion of exuberant feasting, as seen in the above painting by 16th-century Flemish artist Joris Hoefnagel.

"All the world's a stage, / And all the men and women merely players; / They have their exits and their entrances; / And one man in his time plays many parts, / His acts being seven ages."
As You Like It (II, vii)

these fairy creatures, investing them instead with a relatively harmless spirit of mischief. Titania's court is peopled with the delightfully named sprites Peaseblossom, Cobweb, Moth, and Mustardseed—parts assigned to boys with a talent for singing and dancing.

In contrast, witches remained objects of fear, though it is true that England had little acquaintance with the ghoulish imagery common in continental Europe of witches' sabbaths and nightly devil worship. In England witches were old women suspected of casting spells on cattle and preparing evil potions for bridegrooms. They were the "Weird Sisters" of *Macbeth,* the embodiment of absolute evil and witnesses to a revived interest in magic.

The beliefs about witches had their roots in the rural way of life, as well as in a residual paganism that the Reformation had failed to eradicate. The Stuart monarchy was eager to preserve the old myths, with their mysterious, even obscurantist, qualities, and during the Restoration (the period when the monarchy was restored to power following the collapse of the Puritan protectorate) the composer Henry Purcell (c. 1659–95) revived several of them in his "semi-operas" *King Arthur* and *The Fairy Queen,* an elaboration of *A Midsummer Night's Dream.*

The supernatural

The sprite in this 1639 illustration (below) is Robin Goodfellow, also known as Puck; he dances as his companions circle around him. He is portrayed as a satyr, with blatant sexual features and devilish qualities. The Puritans saw such creatures of Celtic folklore as manifestations of the devil.

haunted Shakespeare's plays as it haunted the minds of his contemporaries. Shakespeare's other influences included the Roman playwright Seneca and the Elizabethan theater, including works such as *The Spanish Tragedy* (1587) by Thomas Kyd (1558–94). The sense of terror that seized the audience on the appearance of the ghost of Hamlet's father—an apparition much closer to a pagan specter than to a soul from purgatory—allowed the actor playing the role (probably Shakespeare himself) to utter the lines of his great speech amid a stunned silence. The use of beings from the other world was thus an effective way for the playwright-actor to quiet rowdy audiences.

Sacke & Sugar

Marriage and the "Lost" Years

After leaving school Shakespeare was no doubt an apprentice in the family glove business for a time. Under the date 28 November 1582, when he was just eighteen, we find Shakespeare's name recorded in a legal document next to that of an Anne Hathaway. The bishop of Worcester

Jarmara

Vinegar tom

This watercolor of a witch is from a 1621 treatise on demonology. Witches had devilish attendants who sucked their blood and gave them magic powers in exchange. Thus Joan of Arc at the end of *Henry VI, Part 1* invokes: "Now, ye familiar spirits that are cull'd / Out of the powerful regions under earth, / Help me this once, that France may get the field…. / Where I was wont to feed you with my blood, I'll lop a member off and give it you" (V, iii). And in *Macbeth* Lady Macbeth calls: "Come, you spirits / That tend on mortal thoughts, unsex me here; / And fill me, from the crown to the toe, top-full / Of direst cruelty…. / Come to my woman's breasts, / And take my milk for gall, you murd'ring ministers" (I, v).

had granted him a dispensation to marry this daughter of a farmer from Shottery, near Stratford. She was eight years older than her husband and three months pregnant (hence the need for a dispensation). On about 23 May 1583 a daughter, Susanna, was born to the couple, followed less than two years later by twins, Judith and Hamnet, who were baptized on 2 February 1585.

At this point we lose all trace of Shakespeare for a period of about eight years. The antiquarian John Aubrey (1626–97) relates in *Brief Lives* that Shakespeare became a country schoolmaster, no doubt meaning that he worked as a tutor for a noble family. Other

A stage has been set up by strolling players (below). A few privileged souls are able to watch the play from the window of a nearby tavern. This 16th-century engraving by Pieter Brueghel shows St. George's Day festivities. The primitive stage construction is probably similar to the type used in Shakespeare's childhood days in Stratford.

The engravings of morris dancers on these pages are from an 18th-century edition of Shakespeare's works.

The Spanish Tragedie:

OR,

Hieronimo is mad againe.

Containing the lamentable end of *Don Horatio*, and *Belimperia*; with the pittifull death of *Hieronimo*.

Newly corrected, amended, and enlarged with new Additions of the *Painters* part, and others, as it hath of late been diuers times acted.

LONDON,

In the most memorable scene of Thomas Kyd's *The Spanish Tragedy* (title page, left) the old Hieronimo finds his son hanging in a bower in the garden, and bitter vengeance is set in motion. Feigning madness, Hieronimo uses the device of a play within a play to murder the culprits. This drama was very popular and had a great influence on Shakespeare, as can be seen specifically in his plays *Titus Andronicus* and *Hamlet*.

This drawing of a woman in an Elizabethan bonnet and ruff may be of Anne Hathaway.

sources, relying on poet and dramatist William Davenant (1606–68), claim that he worked in a London theater, first tending horses at the door and then assisting the prompter. Another theory seems more likely: that Shakespeare attached himself to a theatrical company—perhaps the Queen's Men, which happened to have lost one of its members in a brawl. The young Shakespeare could easily have stepped into his shoes, as experience was not required. Actors learned on the job.

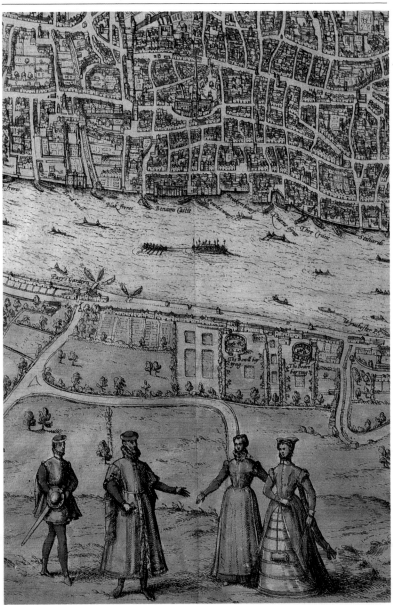

By 1592 Shakespeare had established himself in London, caught up in the capital's astonishing growth. This once small city, numbering some 50,000 in the reign of Henry VIII (ruled 1509–47), underwent a huge influx from the countryside to become a metropolis of 200,000 under Elizabeth I (ruled 1558–1603). Overpopulated and filthy, London was a city of seething activity, spectacle, and theater.

CHAPTER II
LONDON

On Sundays crowds gathered to listen to the sermon at St. Paul's Cathedral, the subject of this anonymous painting (right) dated 1616. This detail from a 1572 map of London (opposite) shows closely packed buildings intersected by thoroughfares, with gardens and open spaces on the outskirts.

In the late 16th century England's capital was confined to an area known as the City, bordered by the Thames to the south and enclosed by a semicircular wall running from Fleet Ditch in the west to the Tower of London in the east. Within these boundaries lay a labyrinth of little streets crossed by two main thoroughfares, one running east-west from Newgate to Aldgate and passing through the districts of Cheapside, Cornhill, and Leadenhall, the other leading from Bishopsgate in the north to London Bridge in the south.

The bridge was the only route across the Thames, apart, of course, from the numerous boats that shuttled between its banks. The bulk of the 200,000-strong population was crammed inside the City walls. On the top of a hill east of Ludgate stood the old St. Paul's Cathedral, dominating the town amid a forest of church towers. The area around St. Paul's was the publishing district, where Shakespeare lived for a time. Shopkeepers and craftspeople ran their businesses in the City, which was ruled by a lord mayor. This dignitary was elected each year by the

The south bank of the Thames (foreground) was mostly open fields in 1588, when the watercolor below was painted, showing the infamous district of Bankside and its arenas for animal fights, next to which the Rose and Globe theaters were built. On the north bank, from east to west, one sees the Tower of London inside its own walls, London Bridge,

LONDON.

and the profile of St. Paul. Farther west are the palaces of the nobility, reaching as far as Westminster, identifiable by its towers, visible at the bottom of the page.

twelve guilds, each of which was highly protective of its privileges. The houses and palaces of the nobility —Somerset House, the Savoy, and the royal palace and gardens of Whitehall—all lay along the banks of the river as far west as Westminster.

When Shakespeare moved there London was in the throes of expansion. Artisans and shopkeepers were still quite strictly regulated and were entrusted with the care of their employees, who often lived with them. Work was grueling, with long hours and few distractions—inside the City gates, at any rate—as the City fathers maintained a close watch over public morals. Theaters and other places of entertainment

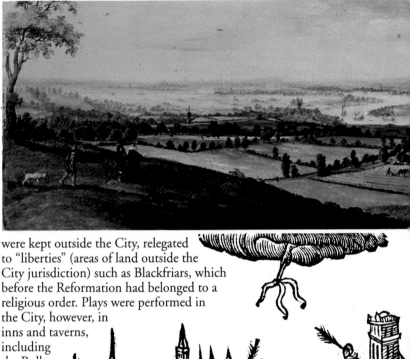

were kept outside the City, relegated to "liberties" (areas of land outside the City jurisdiction) such as Blackfriars, which before the Reformation had belonged to a religious order. Plays were performed in the City, however, in inns and taverns, including the Bull, the Bell, and the Cross Keys, recognizable by their brightly painted signs.

London's southern border, the Thames, abounded in fish and was considered the glory and wealth of the city. More than a river, it was London's main thoroughfare and carried much traffic, from royal barges and large ships to a multiplicity of smaller boats and skiffs belonging to the townspeople.

Seen from Greenwich, London appears a distant blur behind the Isle of Dogs in the center of this Flemish painting dated 1620. Although the country came up to the city gates, and there were numerous gardens within the city's walls, nothing could stop the ravages of the plague, the suffering and death. The only treatment, other than bleeding, was thought to be rosemary, which people would put in their ears and noses to protect themselves. Contaminated houses were boarded up and branded with a red cross, their occupants cut off from the outside world whether or not they were ill. In *Romeo and Juliet* Friar John is prevented from delivering a letter to Romeo, telling him of the stratagem of Juliet's pretended death, because guards at Mantua "Suspecting that we both were in a house / Where the infectious pestilence did reign, / Sealed up the doors, and would not let us forth" (V, ii).

The country was not far off: There were Chelsea, Moorfields, Finsbury Fields—a good place for archery practice—and Paddington, a popular destination for a Sunday walk on the green. And westward along the Strand, as far as the hamlet of Whitehall, parks and gardens were laid out around the palaces.

The Plague

As increasing numbers of people flocked to London from the country, fields and gardens inside City walls became building sites, compounding the problems of sanitation and paving the way for the plague.

The epidemic was seen as the scourge of God on the wickedness of the city. Theaters were immediately closed, the first victims of measures taken more as a step toward moral order than as effective disease prevention. The plague ravaged London in 1564, 1592–3, 1603, and 1623, leaving a total of some 100,000 victims in its wake. Death spread from the suburbs to the city center. Bells rang as the carts went by, carrying corpses to their paupers' graves.

Outside the City walls theaters, brothels, and bear gardens (where one could be "entertained" by cockfights, dogfights, and bear- and bull-baiting) stood side by side. Here, in an atmosphere of carefree anarchy, lived a disreputable crowd of beggars, pickpockets, and peddlers. The area was reputed to be dangerous at particular times of day, though in fact crime seems to have been no greater than it was inside London. To come here one had to pass below the walls of the Tower of London, which held political

prisoners as well as the royal menagerie, with its famous lions and an Indian transported from America. One also had to cross London Bridge—then a bridge spanning twenty arches—along the path for pedestrians and vehicles that ran between the buildings.

Shakespeare "Shake-scene"

The trail of Shakespeare's life, lost after the record of the baptism of his twins in 1585, reappears indirectly in 1592 in the form of a pamphlet written by

People accused of treason were imprisoned in the Tower of London. The impressive fortress with a grim history is shown in this 17th-century engraving (left) by Wenceslaus Hollar. It is to the Tower that the Duke of Clarence in *Richard III* is sent by his brother Edward IV; it is in the Tower that another brother, the Duke of Gloucester, has him murdered. Gloucester also orders the murder of Edward's sons to clear the path to the throne and advises the crown prince, "some day or two / Your highness shall repose you at the Tower," drawing the reply "I do not like the Tower, of any place: / Did Julius Caesar build that place, my lord?" (III, i). In the Renaissance the Tower also housed the royal menagerie.

London Bridge (opposite), once the only route over the Thames, carried rows of houses and shops down each side. The heads of traitors were exhibited on stakes over Bridge Gate (far right) as a reminder of the weight of royal justice.

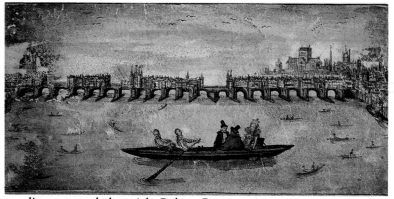

novelist, poet, and playwright Robert Greene (1558–92). Greene gives unique evidence of the young Shakespeare's successful career and much information on the theatrical world of the time, including the rivalries that existed between actors and playwrights and, most of all, between the various companies of players.

In *Groatsworth of Wit Bought with a Million of Repentance,* published three months after his death,

This view of London Bridge (above) is dated c. 1615, the engraving (below), 1616. In 1599 the Swiss traveler Thomas Platter reported that he had crossed the river with friends and, in a building with a thatched roof (the Globe), had seen *Julius Caesar.*

Warke

King Henry the Sixt.

This battell fares like to the mornings Warre,
When dying clouds contend, with growing light
What time the shepherd blowing of his nailes,
Can neither call it perfect day, nor night.
Now swayes it this way, like a Mighty Sea,
Forc'd by the Tide, to combat with the Winde:
Now swayes it that way, like the selfe-same Sea,
Forc'd to retyre by fury of the Winde.
Sometime, the Flood prevailes, and then the Winde:
Now, one the better, then another best;
Both tugging to be Victors, brest to brest:
Yet neither Conqueror, nor Conquered.
So is the equall poise of this fell Warre.

Greene attacks Shakespeare as "an upstart crow, beautified with our feathers" and goes on to refer in even more extreme terms to his "Tygers heart wrapt in a Players hide." This is a parody of the line in Shakespeare's *Henry VI, Part 3* where the Duke of York addresses Queen Margaret, "O tiger's heart wrapp'd in a woman's hide!" (I, iv).

Greene further asserts that "he [Shakespeare] is as well able to bumbast out a blanke verse as the best of you; and being an absolute *Johannes Factotum,* is in his owne conceit the onely Shake-scene in a countrie"—an obvious insult, as well as a rather poor pun on Shakespeare's name.

Left: A modern pastiche recalling a page from the First Folio, the original collection of Shakespeare's plays.

In Shakespeare's day there were no newspapers, and the writer's craft was not profitable. Besides sponsorship by the court, the only path to success was to produce plays capable of drawing large audiences. One such success was the story of the learned Doctor Faustus (below), who, tired of study and yearning to discover the secrets of the universe, sells his soul to the devil in exchange for worldly power and pleasure.

The Tragicall Hiſtor
of the Life and Death
of Doctor FAVSTVS.

With new Additions.

Written by *Ch. Mar.*

Opposite: A 1622 engraving.

Contemporaries, Friends, and Masters

Shakespeare did not simply appear from nowhere in a literary desert. By the 16th century the theater had become an institution, and a group of educated young people set out to make it their career. The first of these was John Lyly

(1544–1606), author also of mannered novels whose main character, Euphues, gave his name to the florid rhetorical style known as euphuism. Lyly's plays are mythological entertainments, for example, *Endimion* (1591) and *Gallathea* (1592), or comedies full of folklore, such as *Mother Bombie* (1594). Performed by companies of boys, these plays were highly successful at court.

Another dramatist and player, George Peele (1556–96), is best known for two works, *The Arraignment of Paris* (1584), a pastoral comedy in the form of a masque, and *The Old Wives' Tale* (1595), which employs the device of a play within a play and is also interesting

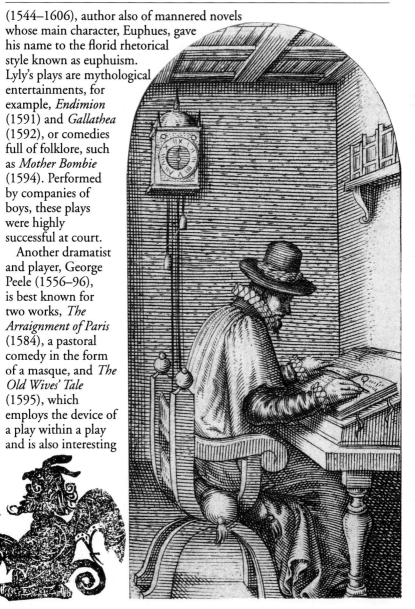

for its use of chivalric elements. The plays of Shakespeare's unhappy rival Robert Greene combined historical tales with fantasy, interweaving several strands of plot and subplot.

But the flourishing of Elizabethan drama was due above all to Thomas Kyd (c. 1557–95) and Christopher Marlowe (1564–93), both of whom wrote tragedies of high drama and emotion. Marlowe's lines, delivered by an actor of the caliber of Edward Alleyn (1566–1626), for example, would resound through the pit of the Rose Theatre. Marlowe's death at the age of twenty-eight—he was stabbed in the eye during a tavern brawl—put a brutal end to a highly promising career. His heroes, the conquering Tamburlaine, the visionary Doctor Faustus, driven by the desire to push back the frontiers of knowledge and the human condition, made Marlowe the very incarnation of Renaissance man.

Kyd's play *The Spanish Tragedy* was a revenge tragedy, the first in a genre that many, including Shakespeare, would take up after him. Its hero, old Hieronimo, feigns madness and uses a theatrical performance as a stratagem to achieve a vengeance as spectacular as it is bloody.

These playwrights knew success before Shakespeare arrived on the scene. But the premature death of Marlowe left the field open and gave the man from Stratford every opportunity, as Greene declared in his pamphlet, to beautify himself with the feathers of his illustrious predecessors.

Shakespeare's Astonishing Rise

A member of the best theatrical company of the time, and free of rivals early on, Shakespeare could look forward to an immediate and undiluted success. His

The portrait opposite, dated 1585, is said to be of Christopher Marlowe. When Shakespeare arrived in London, it was Marlowe's powerful lines that filled the Rose Theatre. The son of a Canterbury cobbler, Marlowe was a precocious genius who had written major works by the age of twenty-seven. His early death may have been politically motivated, as he was employed by the crown as a spy. Shakespeare stepped into his shoes as a dramatist. The three parts of *Henry VI* show him to have been strongly influenced by Marlowe's superb oratorical style. Above is the so-called Chandos portrait of Shakespeare.

Executions were held in public on a raised platform, as seen in this engraving taken from the first edition (1577) of Raphael Holinshed's *Chronicles*. The condemned were entitled to make a speech to the crowd before they died: A bloody form of theater that Shakespeare made use of in *Henry VI* and *Richard III*.

rise marked the triumph of a new generation of professionals in the theater.

The Merchant

Between 1590 and 1597 Shakespeare wrote principally historical dramas. These fall into two tetralogies, the first of which comprises *Henry VI, Parts 1–3,* and *Richard III,* and the second *Richard II, Henry IV, Parts 1–2,* and *Henry V.* He also wrote the single play *King John,* set in the early 12th century. For these dramas Shakespeare found his inspiration in the work of contemporary historian Raphael Holinshed (d. c. 1580), author of *Chronicles of England, Scotland and Ireland.* These were published in 1577 and reissued in 1587 with

illustrations and marginalia intended to make them more attractive and easier to use.

Overlapping with these history plays, between

1593 and 1600, Shakespeare put onto the stage ten comedies, which range from farce to romance: *The Comedy of Errors, Two Gentlemen of Verona, Love's Labour's Lost, A Midsummer Night's Dream, The Taming of the Shrew, The Merchant of Venice, Much Ado About Nothing, As You Like It, The Merry Wives of Windsor,* and *Twelfth Night.*

In the tragic mode he meanwhile produced only *Titus Andronicus,* a bloody revenge tragedy inspired by Seneca and Kyd, and *Romeo and*

M any of Shakespeare's comedies originate in farcical tales in which the world is turned inside out. In *The Taming of the Shrew* Petruchio has to find a way of subduing his wife's temper. Others, notably *The Merchant of Venice,* deal with more serious subjects, such as the nature of justice. There we see the moneylender Shylock ready to take his pound of flesh from the body of the merchant Antonio, who is unable to repay his debt of a thousand ducats.

B elow: A Venetian gondola.

Juliet, a drama of passion and comedy that ends unhappily. With rare exceptions, Shakespeare never invented the plots or characters of his plays. Apart from folklore, he found his subjects in the writings of others, although he was always ready to make major changes to suit the story to the stage and increase its dramatic impact. This approach also enabled him to tackle the burning issues and topical themes of his day, from national history to romantic intrigue, vengeance, madness, or witchcraft. The resounding success of most of his works confirmed that his talent served him well.

Shakespeare: Actor, Writer, and Shareholder

Greene's attack on Shakespeare had its roots in the rivalries plaguing Lord Strange's Men, the troupe to which Shakespeare belonged, which was then playing in the Rose Theatre, owned by a Philip Henslowe. In the detailed accounting journal of performances and profits kept by Henslowe, he mentions two plays by Greene: a comedy, *The Honourable History of Friar Bacon and Friar Bungay,* performed on 19 February 1592, and a tragedy, *Orlando Furioso,* performed shortly

thereafter. Neither work seems to have been popular. In contrast, on 3 March he mentions a play that, to judge by the money taken in, was an outright success: "harey the vi," probably *Henry VI, Part 2.*

Unfortunately, on the heels of these glorious beginnings a violent epidemic of the plague broke out in London. Public theaters were again closed by the City authorities; the existing troupes were disbanded, and the actors scattered. Forced to give up the theater for a while, Shakespeare wrote two narrative poems, *Venus and Adonis* and *The Rape of Lucrece,* dedicating both to his patron Henry Wriothesley, earl of Southampton (1573–1624).

The portrait opposite is of Ferdinando, Lord Strange, the fifth earl of Derby, whose company of players performed *Henry VI* at the Rose Theatre, according to Henslowe's accounts (extract above).

Top: A battle scene dated c. 1615. Left: A 1610 engraving of the Gorgons.

The story of the two cruelly fated lovers Pyramus and Thisbe, portrayed in this engraving dated 1538, is told by Ovid in *Metamorphoses*. It inspired Geoffrey Chaucer (1342–1400) and later Shakespeare, who wrote his first, tragic, version of the same basic story in *Romeo and Juliet*, followed by the burlesque rendering in the play presented to Theseus' court by a group of craftsmen at the end of *A Midsummer Night's Dream*. A playwright had to master every register, to move from laughter to tears, as Shakespeare did, by simple changes of perspective and atmosphere.

He returned to the stage when the theaters reopened in 1594 as one of a company called the Chamberlain's Men. With him were the actors William Kemp and Richard Burbage, among others. They put on two performances of Shakespeare's *The Comedy of Errors* for the court during the Christmas festivities. (Lord Strange had died on 16 April 1593, and in 1594 his theater company passed into the hands of the lord chamberlain, Henry Care. The troupe based itself at the Theatre, James Burbage's playhouse in Bishopsgate, north of the city walls, and severed its connection with Philip Henslowe and the popular actor Edward Alleyn, the star of Marlowe's tragedies. These two men then shifted their allegiance to the lord admiral, Lord Howard of Effingham, and established themselves at the Rose Theatre.)

The Chamberlain's Men were organized in an unusual manner: The six main actors formed an association in which each was a shareholder, directly receiving part of the profits from performances. The actors were financially independent, paying only rent to the theater proprietor. This was in contrast to the Admiral's Men, where the actors were paid by Henslowe, who advanced them money to keep a tighter rein on them. Shakespeare never changed companies again. From this point on he worked to solidify his position as both player and playwright. In addition to acting he wrote an average of two plays a year until 1608, when the pace of theatrical production slackened. The decision early in his career to remain in one place, with one company, enabled him to quickly consolidate his first successes as a writer and to become in his lifetime the most highly sought-after dramatist of the Elizabethan and Jacobean stage.

LVCRECE.

LONDON.
Printed by Richard Field, for Iohn Harrison, and are to be sold at the signe of the white Greyhound in Paules Churh yard. 1594.

Shakespeare's interest in tragedy was already apparent in the dark themes of his poem *The Rape of Lucrece* (1594, above).

Left: Title page of *Titus Andronicus*, 1594.

THE
MOST LA
mentable Romaine
Tragedie of Titus Andronicus:

As it was Plaide by the Right Ho-
neurable the Earle of *Darbie*, Earle of *Pembrooke*,
and Earle of *Suffex* their Seruants.

LONDON,

The drawing below left, dated 1595, is the only contemporary illustration of a scene from Shakespeare's plays. It appears on a page bearing some forty lines of *Titus Andronicus*. In the center the queen of the Goths, Tamora, begs Titus to spare the life of her two sons. On the right the Moor Aaron stands with a sword in his left hand. The costumes worn by Titus and Tamora are vaguely historical, while those of the guards are Elizabethan.

A Wealthy Man

The man whom Greene had termed an upstart soon showed a taste for wealth. He had a keen eye for profit and mercilessly pursued any defaulting debtors. Shakespeare's name appears on tax registers and in a variety of legal disputes with his neighbors. This is how we know that from 1599 he lived for a time on the other side of the Thames, in Southwark, near the new Globe Theatre; he is listed on the bishop of Winchester's registers as a negligent taxpayer.

In 1602 Shakespeare bought roughly 125 acres of land, and in 1605 he bought a share in the Stratford tithe farm for the fairly considerable sum of £440, which was to bring him some £60 per year. In addition, his poetry had earned him the generosity of his patron, the earl of Southampton,

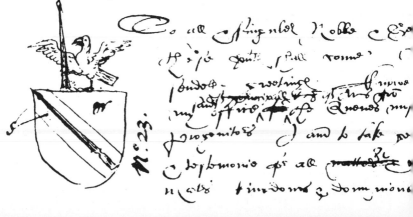

NON SANZ DROICT

who is said to have given him £1000 for *Venus and Adonis* and *The Rape of Lucrece*. This was an enormous sum for the time, and the theater must have brought him even greater rewards. Penniless when he left his native town, Shakespeare found himself some twenty-five years later enjoying one of the largest fortunes in Stratford.

The Gentleman Player

In 1596 Shakespeare applied for the right to bear a coat of arms, renewing the application that had been made by his father, without success, more than twenty-five years earlier. This desire for social recognition was not unusual: A number of actors in William Shakespeare's company—Burbage, Heminge, Cowley, and Pope—had been granted coats of arms, as had Richard Quiney, a Stratford native, whose son Thomas married Shakespeare's daughter Judith in 1616.

This time the Shakespeare family obtained its armorial bearings. The rough draft preserved at the College of Arms shows that the petition was granted in recognition of "the good and loyal service" rendered to the crown by the family's forebears. Through his great success in the theater, Shakespeare, the grandson of a farmer, was now a London gentleman.

Henry Wriothesley, earl of Southampton (opposite), was the patron to whom Shakespeare dedicated the poems written in the months when the theaters were shut down because of the plague. The coat of arms granted to Shakespeare, shown above and in the document below, dated 1598, was "in a field of gold upon a bend sable [black band], a spear of the first, the point upward, headed argent [silver]," the crest "a falcon, with his wings displayed, standing on a wreath of his colours," with the motto "Non sanz droict."

Gentleman, playwright, actor, one of the Chamberlain's Men—Shakespeare knew how to exploit the resources of contemporary theater to the full. The variety of settings, the wealth of dramatis personae, the heterogeneous nature of the audiences—all were in place for the production of his greatest works.

CHAPTER III

THE WORLD OF THEATER

This 18th-century watercolor of the Globe (opposite) was made from a 1616 engraving. Carved on the front of the theater was a quotation from Petronius: "Totus mundus agit histrionem," or, in Shakespeare's words, "All the world's a stage." In this portrait (right) of Tom Skelton, dated c. 1659–65, he wears the traditional motley dress of a jester.

London, where the permanent playhouses were built—the Theatre, the Curtain, and later the Rose, the Swan, the Globe, and the Fortune—had overtaken the provinces, where the mysteries, morality plays, and interludes had developed. A break with the past was made definitively, although not many good plays were performed until 1584. Between 1584 and 1593 the masterpieces were Marlowe's *Tamburlaine* and Kyd's *The Spanish Tragedy*.

The Theatre and the Curtain Theatre, north of the city walls, were the oldest. They belonged to James Burbage, a carpenter. On the other side of the Thames, west of Southwark, Philip Henslowe built the Rose Theatre in 1587. Following in Henslowe's footsteps, Francis Langley, a goldsmith, built the Swan in 1595. This theater was without a resident company, however, and had difficulty competing with the Admiral's Men and the Chamberlain's Men. It was closed down after a performance

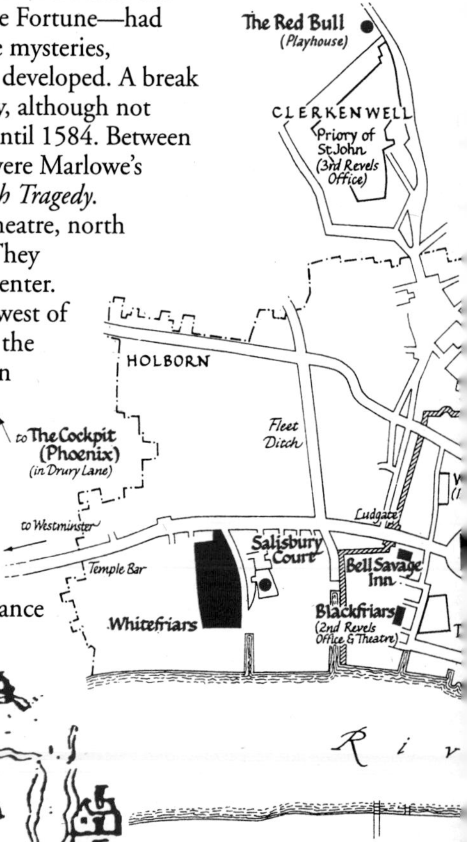

The Red Bull
(Playhouse)

CLERKENWELL
Priory of
St.John
(3rd Revels
Office)

HOLBORN

to The Cockpit
(Phoenix)
(in Drury Lane)

Fleet
Ditch

to Westminster

Ludgate

Temple Bar

Salisbury
Court

Bell Savage
Inn

Whitefriars

Blackfriars
(2nd Revels
Office & Theatre)

R i v

le Playe houle

● The Swan

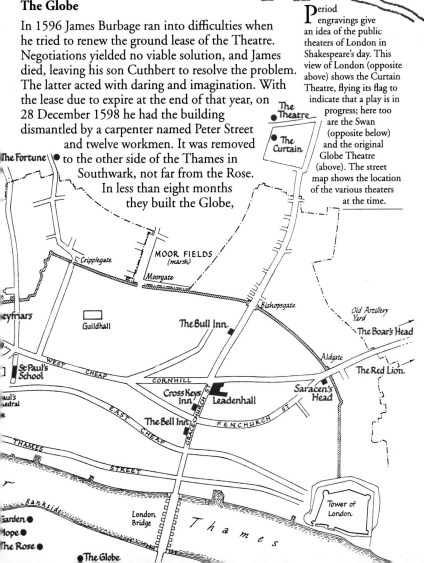

in July 1597, by Lord Pembroke's company, of Thomas Nashe's *The Isle of Dogs,* a play regarded as seditious.

The Globe

In 1596 James Burbage ran into difficulties when he tried to renew the ground lease of the Theatre. Negotiations yielded no viable solution, and James died, leaving his son Cuthbert to resolve the problem. The latter acted with daring and imagination. With the lease due to expire at the end of that year, on 28 December 1598 he had the building dismantled by a carpenter named Peter Street and twelve workmen. It was removed to the other side of the Thames in Southwark, not far from the Rose. In less than eight months they built the Globe,

Period engravings give an idea of the public theaters of London in Shakespeare's day. This view of London (opposite above) shows the Curtain Theatre, flying its flag to indicate that a play is in progress; here too are the Swan (opposite below) and the original Globe Theatre (above). The street map shows the location of the various theaters at the time.

the splendid "wooden O" mentioned by the chorus at the beginning of *Henry V.* A new type of association was formed between the owner of the land, Sir Nicholas Brend, the two Burbage brothers, Cuthbert and Richard (the actor), and the five players in the chamberlain's company. Shakespeare thus became a "householder," or an owner of a share in the property.

The following year, 1600, suffering from the competition provided by the Globe, Philip Henslowe too made a move across the Thames—in the opposite direction. He built the Fortune Theatre to the north of Cripplegate, in the liberty of Finsbury, on a piece of land that his son-in-law, the actor Edward Alleyn, had bought in 1599. Then in 1613 Henslowe embarked on another major building project, turning

This 17th-century engraving is of bull-baiting, a popular sport. In *Troilus and Cressida* the satirical Thersites, watching the fight between Paris and Menelaus, cries, "The cuckold and the cuckold-maker are at it. Now, bull! now, dog! 'Loo, Paris, 'loo!" (V, vii).

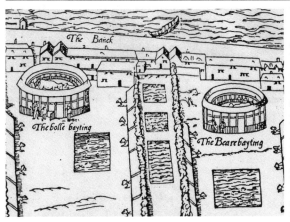

The Banck

The bolle bayting

The Beare bayting

Watercolor of the Globe (opposite) by George Shepherd.

Bear-baiting (below) is another frequent source for Shakespeare's imagery. The bear was tethered to a stake in the ring, into which dogs were released for the attack. A bear might kill a number of the dogs before falling prey to their jaws. A 16th-century map (left) shows two of the arenas used for the sport. In *Julius Caesar* Octavius cries to Anthony, "We are at the stake, / And bay'd about with many enemies" (IV, i). And in *Macbeth,* when Macbeth is cornered by Malcolm's army, his words evoke the same image: "They have tied me to a stake; I cannot fly, / But bear-like I must fight the course" (V, vii).

the bear-baiting arena in west Bankside into the Hope, a theater that could be used for both animal fights and theatrical performances.

The Architecture of Public Theaters

By an order of the Puritan Parliament, all theaters were destroyed in the 1640s. Architectural historians attempting to reconstruct them have had to extract what information they can from drawings, sketches, contracts, and any other documents that have survived.

Each theater had the same basic structure, consisting of a stage partially covered by a thatched roof supported by two pillars. A playhouse averaged forty feet in height and was round or octagonal in shape, with a diameter of about eighty feet. Allowing for a depth of roughly thirteen feet for the three-tiered galleries and boxes, the auditorium itself could not have occupied much more than sixty-five feet, into which space there projected, by

Het Haene gefecht Jn

geLandt .

about twenty-five feet, a raised rectangular stage approximately forty feet wide. The cramped dimensions are striking. No more than twelve actors could appear on the stage at a time because of the space restrictions, yet the Fortune, the Globe, and the Theatre were able to accommodate audiences of between two and three thousand.

The roof of Shakespeare's theater was embellished with a globe, and the front displayed the Latin inscription "Totus mundus agit histrionem" (roughly, "All the world's a stage"). The stage projected into an

It is to a Dutchman, Arend van Buchell, that we owe this drawing (below) of the Swan Theatre, realized from a sketch that his friend Johannes de Witt made in 1596. Van Buchell observed that "the largest and most remarkable of the theaters in London is the Swan, which is able to accommodate three thousand spectators."

uncovered central area within the covered enclosure, which was made up of three tiers of galleries with actors' dressing rooms at the back. The gallery above the stage was independent of the rest and could be used either by the audience or the musicians or as an additional part of the stage (for the balcony scene in *Romeo and Juliet,* for example). The front of the actors' dressing area was broken by two doors for entrances and exits. In the stage floor there was a trapdoor for devilish apparitions, disappearances, and burials. A balcony crowned by a gable on the floor above housed the stage machinery. It was from here that gods, goddesses, and other supporting characters and effects descended onto the stage. When a play was in progress, the theater flew a flag bearing its emblem above the roof.

The Elizabethan Stage

In Shakespeare's day theater relied on convention rather than illusion, using a limited number of portable props, scrupulously inventoried by

The Globe was subject to greater constraints than the more sophisticated Rose Theatre (reconstruction above), judging from the prologue of *Henry V*: "...may we cram / Within this wooden O the very casques / That did affright the air at Agincourt?" Below: A drawing, possibly of a stage set, by Philip Henslowe.

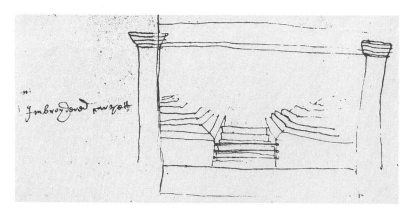

Henslowe in his diary: not only tables, chairs, swords, Cupid's bows, canvases depicting the sun and moon, rocks, and monuments but also a head of Mohammed, a rainbow, Mercury's wand, a tree of golden apples, a series of dragons, and a cauldron for the Jew (a reference to the end of Marlowe's *The Jew of Malta,* in which Barabas is thrown into a cauldron of boiling oil). Scene changes were indicated in the text or by a simple placard. For night scenes, inevitably problematic in an open-air playhouse, a candle or torch symbolically transported the audience into the nocturnal world. As the chorus says at the beginning of *Henry V,* the theater relies

English physician Robert Fludd (1574–1637) produced strange engravings of imaginary stage sets such as the one below, perhaps inspired by the Globe. The images are mnemonic: The five doors onto the stage are intended to recall five texts that one wishes to remember. The five circles and lozenges on the floor are more mysterious.

more on the "imaginary forces" of the audience than on realistic effects. The text sufficed to bring the play to life. Thus, in *King Lear,* for example, Edgar convinces his blind father, Gloucester, that he is on the edge of a cliff (from which Gloucester intends to jump) by describing what is supposedly visible below—crows no bigger than insects, men the size of mice: "How fearful / And dizzy 'tis to cast one's eyes so low! / The crows

"When we are born, we cry that we are come / To this great stage of fools."
King Lear (IV, iii)

Opposite left: A modern pastiche of a First Folio illustration.

and choughs that wing the midway air / Show scarce so gross as beetles.… / The fishermen that walk upon the beach / Appear like mice…" (IV, vi). In the empty space, the symbolic void of the stage, the only note of warmth was provided by the magnificence of the costumes.

An orchestra would often accompany a play with a range of sound effects and instruments; drums and trumpets, for example, served to heighten the excitement of battle scenes.

At the end of a performance the actors would often improvise a sung satirical farce, danced in time to a jig.

A theater stage as illustrated in 1632 on the title page of William Alabaster's play *Roxana*.

The Audience

Thanks to the wide range of prices offered by the "box offices" of the time, theaters were places of popular entertainment. Entrance to the "pit"— standing room around the stage—cost only a penny; prices rose to sixpence for seats in the covered galleries. The first were within reach of all pockets, representing scarcely one-twelfth of a London worker's weekly salary. The second were the preserve of rich city merchants and the nobility. (Sixpence also happened to be the price of a quarto edition of a play.)

THE TRAGEDIE OF IVLIVS CÆSAR.

Cæf. Et Tu Brute———— Then fall Cæfar.

Audiences were highly diverse. The Puritans railed against the rogues, pickpockets, and prostitutes to be found in their midst and regarded the theaters as places of ill repute, no better than the neighboring

"Suit the action to the word, the word to the action; with this special observance, that you o'erstep not the modesty of nature; for anything so o'erdone is from the purpose of playing, whose end, both at the first and now, was and is to hold, as 'twere, the mirror up to nature."
Hamlet (III, ii)

"FALSTAFF: I was as virtuously given as a gentleman need to be; virtuous enough: swore little, dic'd not above seven times a week, went to a bawdy house not above once in a quarter ... of an hour."
Henry IV, Part 1 (III, iii)

Left: An illustration of a bawdy house.

brothels. The motley and bustling crowd of spectators ate and drank during the performances and gave free rein to their emotions—roaring with laughter, dissolving into tears. They delighted in language and were stirred by the long speeches delivered in verse by such actors as Alleyn or Burbage, the stars of the Rose and the Globe.

The Actors

Professional actors were a novelty in late-16th-century England and often much admired. Until then players had been amateurs, members of guilds who acted in morality plays and mysteries on Corpus Christi, or traveling jugglers and mimes who performed at fairs and on village greens. In *A Midsummer Night's Dream,* for example, when Bottom and his company rehearse the drama "Pyramus and Thisbe," hoping to be permitted to perform it at court on the occasion of the marriage of Duke Theseus, the actors are all artisans in various fields: weaver, carpenter, tailor, and bellows mender.

King's Men players (left to right): John Lowin, William Sly, and Nathan Field, who probably replaced Shakespeare when he died.

The situation changed when the government began to take measures to control vagrancy and delinquency. An order was passed in 1572 that made an actor into a potential suspect, liable to be thrown into prison and branded with a hot iron if he were caught. This made it essential for a player to join the company of a prominent figure and bear his livery and arms.

The number of principal shareholders in the Chamberlain's Men increased to twelve in 1604, after Queen Elizabeth's death. The company had been taken under the wing of the new sovereign, James I (ruled 1603–25), and become known as the King's Men. The actors had the honor of marching in the celebrations organized for the new king's accession.

The size of each actor's share was proportionate to the sum he had invested in the business for the purchase of the basic stock—props and costumes. The shareholders divided among them half of the income from the gallery seats, while the other half went toward the costs and upkeep of the theater. Though the total obviously varied, it often proved substantial. In addition to the company core, hired men would play minor roles for a weekly salary that was less than the average earnings of a laborer.

"Wee ... doe licence and aucthorize theise our Servauntes Lawrence Fletcher, William Shakespeare, Richard Burbage, Augustyne Phillippes, Iohn Heninges, Henrie Condell, William Sly, Robert Armyn, Richard Cowly, and the rest of theire Assosiates freely to use and exercise the Arte and faculty of playing Comedies, Tragedies, histories, Enterludes, moralls, pastoralls, Stageplaies...."

James I
Letter patent of 1603

This picture (left, c. 1608) may depict John Green, an actor who won fame on his tours in 1607–8.

Others were engaged as watchmen, wardrobe keepers, property men, copyists, musicians, and prompters.

At the time of Shakespeare's death the King's Men consisted of twenty-six permanent actors—a considerable number for the time.

Female Roles

The theatrical companies included five or six boys or adolescents who played female roles until their voices broke. They learned their trade from the most accomplished actors and were well paid as long as the theaters flourished. But their prospects were uncertain: At puberty, when they could no longer wear wigs and dresses, they often had no future other than as humble company employees.

These youths were nonetheless true professionals, who, starting at a very young age, learned singing, dancing, music, diction, and feminine gestures and intonation. Contemporary audiences found them wholly convincing. Their parts were difficult, however, as well as specialized. It is therefore no surprise that, given the preponderance of adults in the companies, Shakespeare's plays have fewer female than male characters.

The Clowns

The clown was another specialized role. On the Elizabethan stage a distinction was made between the clown and the fool. The former was a rough peasant whose blunders served as a counterbalance to the heroic or romantic language

In a comical scene from *A Midsummer Night's Dream* the craftsmen of Athens, eager to perform "Pyramus and Thisbe" at court, seem reluctant to play female parts: "QUINCE: Flute, you must take Thisby on you. FLUTE: What is Thisby? A wand'ring knight?

QUINCE: It is the lady that Pyramus must love. FLUTE: Nay, faith, let not me play a woman; I have a beard coming" (I, ii).

Hostes

of the other characters. The latter was a professional jester fitted out in motley (the colorful garment traditionally associated with jesters), cap, and bells.

In 1588 the clown Richard Tarlton died. The sparkling repartee and humor of this misshapen and flat-nosed dwarf had made him famous throughout London; he amused even the queen. He was replaced by the clown William Kemp, who joined the Chamberlain's Men. Kemp performed marvelously as Launcelot Gobbo in *The Merchant of Venice* and as Dogberry, the stupid constable in *Much Ado About Nothing*. After Kemp

Richard Tarlton, the queen's favorite clown, is portrayed above in peasant dress, playing a pipe and drum, in a drawing of c. 1588 by John Scottowe. The other illustrations are from the title page of *The Wits* (1673) by Francis Kirkman, a collection of comic scenes from popular plays.

left the company in 1600 Shakespeare engaged Robert Armin, a slight, intelligent man, for whom he wrote jesting parts, such as that of Touchstone in *As You Like It,* and roles that displayed an acrobatic wit, one of which was the fool in *King Lear.* By means of his capers and verbal games, the fool gives the king a bitter lesson in wisdom.

The Actor's Art

A combination of talent and dedication was required of all these actors, for the theaters were commercial enterprises dependent on the success of the plays they performed. And competition was fierce. In season—in other words, outside Lent, when the theaters were closed—actors performed every afternoon except on Sunday. They also had

The clown William Kemp danced for nine days on the road from London to Norwich, as illustrated in his book *Nine Daies Wonder* (1600, above). Plays often ended with a dance, and with the audience going off to slake its thirst in a nearby tavern (below). An early 17th-century painting (opposite) by Lady Drury shows a common image of a clown with a set of bellows or, in Latin, *follis*—a form of visual pun.

Etiam asino dormienti.

Dic mihi, qualis eris?

The panels painted by Lady Drury at Hawstead, her house near Bury St. Edmunds in Suffolk, were clearly inspired by engravings in contemporary books of emblems, such as those by Geoffrey Whitney (1586) and Claude Paradin (1591). These compilations all followed the same pattern: One emblem per page, with a Latin motto above, an engraving of moral, allegorical, or enigmatic import in the center, and a brief commentary on the image below. Lady Drury's panels feature only a restrained scroll bearing a Latin saying. The sleeping figure in the panel opposite surely represents sloth, though it can also be seen as an illustration of Bottom, after he is transformed into a donkey in *A Midsummer Night's Dream.* The painting at left calls to mind the central metaphor of Shakespeare's Sonnet 24: "Mine eye hath play'd the painter and hath stell'd / Thy beauty's form in table of my heart / My body is the frame wherein 'tis held, / And perspective it is best painter's art."

Reason in Madness

One of Whitney's emblems was entitled "Aethiopem lavare" ("To wash the Ethiopian"), the moral of which was that one cannot change the color bestowed on one by nature, however hard one tries. This was clearly the inspiration of the panel opposite by Lady Drury. In *Titus Andronicus* Aaron, the evil-minded Moor, defends the color of his skin, or more precisely that of the illegitimate child that Tamora, queen of the Goths, has just had by him: "Coal-black is better than another hue / In that it scorns to bear another hue; / For all the water in the ocean / Can never turn the swan's black legs to white, / Although she lave them hourly in the flood" (IV, ii). The ship about to be capsized by a whale (left above), with the motto "Nusquam tuta fides" ("One cannot rely on promises"), recalls the opening scene in *The Tempest,* where Antonio and the courtiers of Milan discover to their stupefaction that the enraged waves seem only to mock the authority of the king. The old man (left below) beside the motto "Desipui sapiendo" ("Through my wisdom I was foolish") suggests King Lear on the barren heath.

to vary their repertoire regularly and generally had no more than two weeks in which to prepare a new play. Actors often found themselves playing several roles, particularly on tour, when the troupe was reduced to a minimum. This demanded quick work and an excellent memory. In 1594–5 the Admiral's Men performed thirty-eight plays, twenty-one of which were new.

The Public and the Actors

Those who frequented the theater, and in particular the pit—which meant standing throughout "the two hours' traffic" of a performance, as the prologue to *Romeo and Juliet* calls it—were eager for sensation and overwhelming emotion. They loved impassioned grandiloquence, metaphor, and extremes. It was pointless to mumble words to jostling and undisciplined spectators: Their attention had to be captured.

A taste for thrills and horror was deeply embedded in popular audiences. Hence the success of revenge tragedies, rich in macabre scenes and spectacular

There were many books about dueling and its rules written in the Renaissance, among them George Silver's *Paradoxes of Defence* (1599). The illustration of a duel below is from 1616. In the theater duels and combats, for instance, the one between Mercutio and Tybalt in *Romeo and Juliet,* or between Edgar and his half brother Edmund at the end of *King Lear,* were carefully arranged and highly popular with audiences of the period. In comedies such as *As You Like It* and *Twelfth Night,* the duel was presented as a dangerous passion and the absurd fashion of another age.

effects. The strength of national feeling, stirred by the defeat of the Spanish Armada in 1588, and the craze for English history, revealed by the success of a play such as Marlowe's *Edward II,* are further evidenced by the popularity of the highly colored scenes represented in the chronicles and history plays. The din of battle and clash of weapons evoked strong emotion, while heroic deeds were an occasion to show actors in hand-to-hand combat.

Gone were the days of the versatile strolling players, generally limited to four adults and two boys, with each actor playing several parts. The two largest public theaters in London and the private theaters—theaters with covered auditoriums—staged very different plays, each with its particular style and its own "regulars." Edward Alleyn, attached to the Rose and then the Fortune, was famous for his declamatory manner. Shakespeare, on the other hand, wrote psychologically complex parts for Richard Burbage, such as that of the prince in *Hamlet,* who reveals different aspects of his character as the play unfolds. As an actor, Shakespeare was content to play minor roles, for example, that of Adam, the old servant in *As You Like It,* or the king's ghost in *Hamlet.*

Richard Burbage (1568–1619), a talented artist, may have painted this portrait (left) of himself. A son of James Burbage, who built the Theatre, he was a star performer in the Chamberlain's Men. He played all the great parts in Shakespeare's tragedies —Hamlet, Othello, and King Lear. An anecdote recorded in 1602 by the lawyer John Manningham related that when Burbage was playing Richard III, a lady in the audience invited him to her house. Overhearing this, Shakespeare hurried to get there before him. When Burbage arrived at the lady's door, he was informed that William the Conqueror had come before Richard III.

HAMLET, Prince of Denmarke.

Alas poore *Toricke,* I knew him *Horatio*

The *Tragedie of King Lear.*

poore *Tom.* O matter, and impertinency mixt, Reason in Madnesse.

Why Did Shakespeare Not Publish His Plays?

It may be surprising to learn that Shakespeare did not arrange for his plays to be published. That he might have considered them not good enough is unthinkable. Indeed, there is clear evidence of the tremendous reception his work was given by the

Shakespeare was well known among his contemporaries, who often mentioned him with admiration. None of his manuscripts has survived, however.

> As *Plautus* and *Seneca* are accounted the beſt for Comedy and Tragedy among the Latines : ſo *Shakeſpeare* among ẙ Engliſh is the moſt excellent in both kinds for the ſtage;

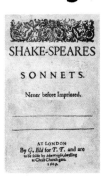

public. Clergyman Francis Meres, in his 1598 critique of English authors, *Palladis Tamia: Wits Treasury,* wrote: "As Plautus and Seneca are accounted the best for Comedy and Tragedy among the Latines: so Shakespeare among [the] English is the most excellent in both kinds for the stage."

The only examples of his work Shakespeare published were *Venus and Adonis* and *The Rape of Lucrece.* Meres felt the "sweete wittie soule" of Ovid live again in these narrative poems. Of the "sugred Sonnets," all he tells us is that they were circulated privately among Shakespeare's friends. They were not published until 1609.

Theater was not yet considered a truly literary genre. It might have provided a fair living, but this did not put it in the same rank as poetry. The text of a play was continually reworked, with a monologue added here or cut there to avoid causing offense; and there was frequent improvisation on the part of the clowns, who often strayed from the script to make the audience laugh. Hamlet goes as far as to remind the strolling players who had come to Elsinore to "let

Above: Extract from Francis Meres's *Wits Treasury* (1598).

Shakespeare intended his plays to be viewed by an audience, not read. The sonnets (title page of the 1609 edition, left), however, were a different matter. In their case the poet declared proudly: "Or I shall live your epitaph to make, / Or you survive when I in earth am rotten; / From hence your memory death cannot take, / Although in me each part will be forgotten. / Your name from hence immortal life shall have, / Though I, once gone, to all the world must die.... / You still shall live, such virtue hath my pen, / Where breath most breathes, even in the mouths of men" (Sonnet 81).

those that play your clowns speak no more than is set down for them, for there be of them that will themselves laugh, to set on some quantity of barren spectators to laugh too" (III, ii). Some passages were also revised after a few performances if they had failed to produce the intended response in the audience.

Below: The title page from one of the "Good Quartos," the reasonably authoritative texts that Shakespeare approved for publication.

A Midsommer nights dreame.

As it hath beene sundry times publickely acted, by the Right honourable, the Lord Chamberlaine his servants.

Written by William Shakespeare.

Imprinted at London, for Thomas Fisher, and are to be soulde at his shoppe, at the Signe of the White Hart, in Fleetestreete. 1600.

In *A Midsummer Night's Dream* the people of Athens get into some bizarre situations: "Thou art as wise as thou art beautiful," says the besotted queen of the fairies to Bottom with his ass's head (left above). "Not so, neither," is his reply (III, i).

Below: The Man i' th' Moon— with his lantern, dog, and faggot— appears at the nighttime meeting of Pyramus and Thisbe.

The First Pirate Editions

Writing under pressure to meet public demand, Shakespeare would have found it impossible to supply a printer with a definitive text. A number of quarto volumes of his plays were nonetheless published in his lifetime. These were either poor editions pirated by unscrupulous people seeking to profit from the success

Shakespeare the Enigma

Who was William Shakespeare? Many critics have sought to prove that the actor Shakespeare cannot have been the author of the brilliant work found in the First Folio of 1623. How could the mere son of a glover have acquired the great classical, juridical, and technical knowledge revealed in his work? Where did he gain his understanding of court circles? The philosopher, author, and politician Francis Bacon (1561–1626), and the earls of Derby, Oxford, and Essex, have all been considered as rival candidates, but none is now taken seriously. These portraits are believed to be of Shakespeare: The "Flower" portrait (opposite); the "Ely Palace" portrait (left above); a portrait in Washington, D.C.'s Folger Library (above); and a portrait attributed to Gerard Soest (left below).

of the stage plays or reasonably reliable texts, as in the case of *Richard II, Love's Labour's Lost, A Midsummer Night's Dream,* or *Henry IV, Part 1.* Known as the "Good Quartos," these were copied from manuscripts and sold to the publisher by the company when it was short of money and when the play in question had reached the end of its run.

Companies were anxious that copies of their plays should not proliferate, for this was the surest way of keeping the performances in their own hands; as soon as a play was published anyone could put it on stage for a profit. Just as the guilds guarded their trade secrets, the troupes controlled the circulation of their manuscripts so as not to lose their audiences in an age when the appetite for novelty was considerable. The playwrights' manuscripts were as much part of a company's stock as the costumes, sets, and props. To sell them without having fully exploited them first would have been remarkably shortsighted.

Playwrights, furthermore, viewed printers and publishers with a wary eye. These professions belonged to the Worshipful Company of Stationers

Printing was introduced to England in 1476 by William Caxton (1422–91), a former silk merchant and diplomat, who established a press at Westminster. The engraving above, dated 1620, shows a press in operation while a typographer in the background arranges the cast-lead letters in a printing form. We know the names of the printers of the quartos of Shakespeare's plays. Unlike Thomas Millington, Thomas Pavier, and John Danter, who published the "Bad Quartos," Andrew Wise, Matthew Law, and Cuthbert Burby published only authorized texts.

The book trade grew up in London in the district of St. Paul's, where Shakespeare lived for a time, and also in Oxford and Cambridge. An edition of a book usually numbered a few hundred, rising to a few thousand in the case of the Bible and other religious works. This engraving of a bookshop dates from 1689. This writer or scholar (below left), who seems to be brandishing his book like a shield, dates from c. 1616. In *Titus Andronicus* it is thanks to a book, Ovid's *Metamorphoses,* that Lavinia is able to put her father on the trail of those who have raped her and cut off her tongue. "TITUS: How now, Lavinia! Marcus, what means this? / Some book there is that she desires to see. / Which is it, girl, of these?—Open them, boy.— / But thou art deeper read and better skill'd: / Come and take choice of all my library, / And so beguile thy sorrow, till the heavens / Reveal the damn'd contriver of this deed" (IV, i).

—incorporated in 1557 under an order signed by Queen Mary—which had sole control of publication rights. After vetting by the official censors, the archbishop of Canterbury and bishop of London, every new work was inscribed in the Stationers' Register, which guaranteed the exclusive right to print and sell a book. The concept of copyright existed, but it was vested in the publisher, not in the author.

The 1623 "First Folio," a collection of Shakespeare's works published by two fellow actors, was printed in an edition of a thousand and sold for £1 a copy. Two hundred survive, fourteen of which are in perfect condition.

Queen Elizabeth I used various symbolic images to present herself to her subjects as the Virgin Queen. She liked to be personified as Diana, Roman goddess of the moon and chaste huntress, or as Astraea, goddess of justice and innocence. Like all writers of the age, Shakespeare portrayed her in terms she would find flattering.

CHAPTER IV

ELIZABETH I: MYTH AND PROPAGANDA

The Spanish Armada, which was launched by King Philip II in 1588 to invade Britain, ended in disaster. Queen Elizabeth was triumphant over the Catholic forces. She is portrayed here (opposite) on a visit to Tilbury, at the mouth of the Thames, to speak to the victorious troops, while the enemy ships blaze in the distance. In contrast to this image of a warrior queen, the miniature at right gives her an air of gentleness.

An entire symbolic bestiary, featuring the phoenix and the pelican, was associated with the queen. The phoenix, an icon of virginity, also expressed her uniqueness, while the pelican symbolized her devotion to her people. Contemporary portraits represent Elizabeth variously holding a rainbow, bearing the olive branch of peace, standing beside a pillar of constancy, or with her hand upon the globe of the earth or the heavens. She is rendered in all her majesty with emblems of both the microcosm and the macrocosm.

A mythology developed around the figure of the queen. Writers such as Sir Walter Raleigh (1554–1618) and Sir John Davies (1569–1626) endowed her with a range of symbolic associations that visibly influenced official paintings of processions, receptions, tournaments, and even the architecture of the period. It was not unheard of for a member of the queen's court to build himself a house in the form of an "E", the initial letter of his sovereign's name.

The royal mythology similarly marked the drama of the Elizabethan age. The comedies Shakespeare wrote between 1595 and 1600 indirectly paid tribute to the queen by creating more important roles for women and giving many of them "feminist" voices: Rosalind in *As You Like It,* for example, who playfully rebukes her suitor, Orlando, or Beatrice in *Much Ado About Nothing,* who meets Benedick's "for truly I love

Following the defeat of the Spanish, anti-Catholic propaganda presented Elizabeth I as the great empress of the world. This anonymous "Armada" portrait (c. 1588) shows her with her right hand resting on the globe. Having vanquished the forces of evil, she appears in all her glory.

One face of this jewel (opposite) by Nicholas Hilliard bears the queen's emblem, the Tudor rose, a sign of chastity. The ark on the back (above) means sanctuary.

Pictures of the Queen

The portraits of Elizabeth on the preceding pages show the extent to which she was the object of a personality cult during her reign. Her dresses and accessories are extraordinarily lavish and richly symbolic, proclaiming the virtues and powers that she embodied. The sieve and feathers that she holds (p. 94, above) and the white flowers on her dress (p. 95) are symbols of chastity. The hand laid on her heart and the rainbow in her hand (p. 94, below) invest her with a luminous radiance. The portrait (p. 95) by Marcus Gheeraerts the Younger was probably painted during a visit to Sir Henry Lee's house. In it the queen is standing on the globe, with her feet pointing to Oxfordshire, where Lee's house was located. Early in her reign the queen was presented in terms of more traditional mythology, as in the anonymous painting at left, where Juno, Athena, and Venus are eclipsed by the arrival of Elizabeth, a new goddess who transcends them in power, wisdom, and beauty.

none" with the retort, "I had rather hear my dog bark at a crow than a man swear he love me" (I, i).

Images of an Ideal Monarchy

The festivities of the Elizabethan court followed a well-ordered calendar, suggesting a world of uninterrupted splendor. Winter was the season of revels, and every 17 November the queen went to Whitehall to celebrate the anniversary of her accession to the throne. Sumptuous tournaments were organized, at which her champions—courtiers like Henry Lee and Robert Ratcliffe—contended for her favors and the privilege of serving her. There were great displays of arms, caparisoned horses, foot servants, and banners flaunting coats of arms and Latin mottos composed in her honor. Next came Christmas festivities, organized by

Elizabeth was a vivacious queen with a taste for feasting and dancing, which she made an important part of court life. In this painting of a banquet (above) she has been identified as dancing the gavotte. The popularity of this pastime is evoked in *Henry V* when the French, driven back by the fierce attack of the English, turn to ironic gallantries: "DAUPHIN: By faith and honour, / Our madams mock at us.... BOURBON: They bid us to the English dancing schools / And teach lavoltas high and swift corantos, / Saying our grace is only in our heels" (III, v).

the court's master of the revels. The entertainment included music, balls, masques, and plays performed by one of the companies of the public theaters or by a group of children from one of the churches.

In the summer the queen moved to the country with her entire court, to be received with much pomp by her vassals, who vied with each other for this costly privilege. Splendid outdoor entertainments were held in her honor, in gardens and on lakes, where boating displays were frequently followed by fireworks.

Palaces and Gardens

The Elizabethan age was marked by an architectural flowering. Buildings acquired an exotic and even bizarre appearance, with a multiplication of tall gables, domes, facades broken by pilasters and colonnades, huge casements and mullioned windows, and the tall chimneys alluded to in Shakespeare's *Henry VI, Part 1.* Neither Italian nor French, this was a peculiarly English Renaissance architecture. Inside, the rooms were many and vast, particularly the huge ceremonial halls with their elaborate timber roof beams. Floors were covered with rushes, and walls were hung with magnificent tapestries depicting pastoral and mythological scenes with floral or animal motifs.

In 1580 pleasure gardens began to come into fashion, with their clipped hedges, flower beds laid out in geometric or symbolic designs, mazes, and fountains. The surprises and wonders that form the backdrop to a comedy such as *A Midsummer Night's Dream* were no doubt influenced by these mannerist gardens, peopled

Elizabeth turned the anniversary of her accession to the throne into a national festival. Church bells rang all day, and the court attended sumptuous tournaments at which knights jousted in honor of the queen (bottom illustrations). This portrait of the earl of Sussex in armor is dated 1593 (below).

0

by strange statues and adorned with hedges cut in the form of heraldic beasts, monsters, and savages.

Gardeners planted their beds with flowers symbolizing purity (roses and daisies) in tribute to the queen, founder of a new "Golden Age." The gardens of the country houses and royal residences—Kenilworth, Theobalds, and Hatfield—were designed on emblematic lines, with hedges cut to represent family coats of arms. It was in these symbolic landscapes that summer pageants were presented. In a nature cunningly shaped by the gardener's hand, Elizabeth found allegories in her own image, tributes to the mark she had made on the era.

Fireworks were a common feature of court entertainments. Sparklers were held in the hand, as shown in this engraving (left) of a man dressed up as a savage.

Microcosm and Macrocosm

Similar to this age's symbolic vision of nature was that of the stars and planets. The Elizabethan concept of the universe was still based on the theories of the Alexandrian astronomer Ptolemy (2nd century AD). In his system the sun and seven planets revolved in concentric spheres around a stationary earth. Below the moon was the world of mutability, above it, that of permanence. At the top lay the firmament and the fiery sphere, to which the stars were fixed like gold nails.

The curious poem below, in the form of a pyramid that reads from top to bottom, is a compliment to Queen Elizabeth.

Skie
Azured
In the
Assur'de
And better
And richer
Much greater

Crownandempir
After an hier
For to aspire
Like flame of fire
In form of Spire

To mount on hie
Con-ti-nu-al-ly
With travel and teen.
Most gracious Queen
Ye have made a vow
Shews us plainly how
Not fained but true
To everyman s vew
Shining cleere in you
Of so bright an-hewe
Even thus vertewe

Vanish out of sight
Till his fine top be quite
To taper in the ayre
Endevours soft and faire.
By his kindly nature.
Of tall comely stature
Like as this faire figure

In 1543 the Polish astronomer Nicolaus Copernicus (1473–1543) published *De Revolutionibus Orbium Coelestium* ("On the revolution of the celestial spheres"), the basis of modern astronomy; but his hypotheses were not

One of Elizabeth's finest palaces was Nonsuch in Surrey, portrayed below by Joris Hoefnagel. It was demolished in 1680.

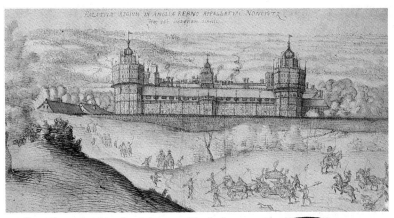

confirmed until 1609 (by Johannes Kepler) and 1610 (by Galileo Galilei). Thus only a few learned Elizabethans knew of his theories, and they formed no part of the consciousness of the age.

Astrology continued to be part of the curriculum of the universities. Traditional medicine linked bodily rhythms and diseases to the motions of the seven planets and the influence of the twelve signs of the zodiac on the parts of the human body. Aries, for example, was thought to rule the head and face, Taurus the neck, Gemini the shoulders, Leo the back and heart, and Cancer the chest, stomach, and lungs.

Furthermore, the movements of the stars and the appearance of comets and eclipses were believed to be portents of disaster. In other words, the human microcosm could be understood only in reference to the macrocosm of all creation. Shakespeare and his

This 16th-century engraving shows Ptolemy's system of the universe with its concentric spheres.

Elizabethan Gardens

Elizabethan gardens were designed according to strict principles. The flower beds were laid out in squares or in knots, intricate patterns that could be emblematic or purely ornamental, as in these early 17th-century garden designs (left and below). This view of a garden (opposite) is a detail of a painting by Joos de Momper, dated 1633. Flowers and vegetables were chosen for their colors and for the season of their blooming or ripening. Hedges were clipped into geometric or animal shapes, and many stately homes had mazes in their gardens. Shakespeare frequently uses the allegory of the enclosed garden, as in *Richard II,* where it serves as a representation of his kingdom: "Why should we, in the compass of a pale, / Keep law and form and due proportion, / Showing, as in a model, our firm estate, / When our sea-walled garden, the whole land, / Is full of weeds; her fairest flowers chok'd up, / Her fruit trees all unprun'd, her hedges ruin'd, her knots disordered, and her wholesome herbs / Swarming with caterpillars?" (III, iv).

contemporaries saw nature as a unified whole, which—however various its manifestations—lent itself to universal interpretation by the laws of analogy and the theory of "signatures." Signatures were outward signs or special marks by which it was believed possible to decipher the essence of things and the universe; they were blazons, or hieroglyphs representing the hidden world, enabling the sage or seer to read the works of God in the great book of nature. Hence the vogue for exempla (rhetorical moral sayings), mottos, books of emblems, and compilations of all the key images and figures that determined the connections between things and relations between humans.

An entire hierarchical system thus linked the different orders of life from minerals to angels, establishing lateral connections between plants and animals at each level or stage of the chain.

Medicine was dominated by the theories of the Greek physician Galen, who lived in the 2nd century AD. He believed there were four humors, or fluids—black bile, phlegm, blood, and choler—that determined the temper of the mind and body. The melancholic humor was cold and dry, like earth, and could produce an excess of black bile; the phlegmatic humor was cold and wet, like water, and came from the kidneys or lungs; the sanguine humor was warm and humid, like air, and originated in the liver, the seat of the passions; lastly, the choleric humor was hot and dry,

R obert Fludd (left) wrote learned treatises on the relationship between the macrocosm (the universe) and the microcosm (humanity). Ulysses in *Troilus and Cressida* shares his view of cosmology: "The heavens themselves, the planets, and this centre, / Observe degree, priority and place, / Insisture, course, proportion, season, form, / Office, and custom, in all line of order.… / O, when degree is shak'd, / Which is the ladder of all high designs, / The enterprise is sick!" (I, iii).

O pposite: This zodiacal manuscript page is dated c. 1480.

B elow: A 1588 engraving showing the queen's symbolic realm.

like fire. Illnesses and nervous disorders were attributed to an imbalance in the humors; an even balance produced a "good humor." Melancholy was the affliction of the age, as can be seen in Shakespeare characters as diverse as Jaques, the moralist; Romeo, the lover; and Hamlet, the prince in mourning.

Medicines were unreliable and somewhat hazardous. They ranged from the traditional, based on herbs and medicinal plants, to the fearsome, an

This c. 1590 portrait of a young dandy by Isaac Oliver conveys the world-weariness voiced by many of Shakespeare's characters, among them Jaques in *As You Like It*: "I have neither the scholar's melancholy, which is emulation; nor the musician's, which is fantastical; nor the courtier's, which is proud; nor the soldier's, which is ambitious; nor the lawyer's, which is politic; nor the lady's, which is nice; nor the lover's, which is all these; but it is a melancholy of mine own, compounded of many simples, extracted from many objects, and, indeed, the sundry contemplation of my travels; in which my often rumination wraps me in a most humorous sadness" (IV, i).

assortment of drugs and ointments containing ingredients such as spider's web, hare's fur, and eggshells. All such remedies proved helpless against epidemics like the plague, however, which ravaged the cities regularly.

These beliefs and the ineffectiveness of medicines encouraged reliance on seers, astrologers, and alchemists such as Simon Forman (1552–1611) and John Dee (1527–1608). The latter, a philosopher, mathematician, and astrologer, wrote almanacs, horoscopes, and predictions. He was much heeded at court and had no small influence on the queen.

While he did not directly serve the monarchy, Shakespeare in his dramatic works nonetheless reflected prevalent beliefs and practices by making his characters refer to them in their speeches. Yet he never reveals himself the slave of any specific ideology or point of view, and the many contradictions that emerge in his plays are only the expression of an infinite diversity of opinion.

Thus in *Troilus and Cressida* (I, iii), for example, Ulysses makes a long speech on the chaos that threatens when the traditional hierarchy, which he calls "degree," is not respected, whereas Gloucester's bastard son Edmund in *King Lear* mocks at astrology and its unreliable predictions: "This is the excellent foppery of the world, that when we are sick in fortune, often the surfeits of our own behaviour, we make guilty of our disasters the sun, the moon, and stars" (I, ii).

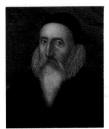

Medicine in Shakespeare's day was not far from torture. The engraving at left shows the treatment for a dislocated shoulder. Birth defects were seen as the work of the devil, and the distinction between the real and the imagined was not always clear to learned men like the astrologer John Dee (above). The child with a frog's head (below) illustrated a surgeon's treatise.

MR. WILLIAM SHAKESPEARES

COMEDIES, HISTORIES, & TRAGEDIES.

Publifhed according to the True Originall Copies.

LONDON

Printed by Iſaac Iaggard, and Ed. Blount. 1623.

Elizabeth I dies, James I succeeds her, and Shakespeare loses any lingering shreds of optimism. Anxiety, uncertainty, and disillusionment hold sway in the theater as Machiavellianism triumphs and all opposition seems in vain. Life is but a masque.

CHAPTER V

A NEW WORLD

King of Scotland since 1567, when his mother, Mary Stuart, was forced to abdicate, James I (1566–1625) became king of England in 1603. This portrait of him (right), dated 1610, is by John de Critz the Elder.

Elizabeth's death caused no setback to Shakespeare: His career, well established by the end of her reign, forged ahead in the Jacobean era. Opposite is the title page of the First Folio, published in 1623.

James I Ascends the Throne

On 24 March 1603 Elizabeth I died.
It was the end of an era and a dynasty.
In the absence of a direct heir, the crown
passed to James VI of Scotland, a Stuart
and distant cousin of the queen's.

James I, as he was to be known in England,
soon took the Chamberlain's Men under his
wing, renaming them the King's Men. The
company reciprocated by putting on eleven
performances between November 1604 and
autumn 1605. Eager to please the new
sovereign, they chose seven
plays by Shakespeare, among

The queen's funeral
took place on 28
April 1603, accompanied
by a solemn procession
(above and below). The
crowd followed the
horses, banners held
high, halberds
pointed to the
ground.
Shortly
afterward, the
plague hit
London anew. Not
until 1604 could
James I (left) safely
enter the city.

which were two
new works, *Measure for Measure* and *Othello*.
The playwright's reputation was then at its
height. Much adulated and enjoying the
patronage of influential friends, he was
called "gentle Shakespeare" or, more
familiarly, "good Will."

A New Genre: "Dark Comedy"

In the period between Elizabeth's last years
and the coronation of James I, Shakespeare

embarked on a new genre, which critics have termed the "problem plays" or "dark comedies." The first of these, begun around 1601, are *Troilus and Cressida* and *All's Well That Ends Well,* ironical and troubled works. He continued in a similar vein in the following years, writing *Measure for Measure, Antony and Cleopatra, Timon of Athens,* and *Coriolanus,* apparently disillusioned by the uncertain political climate.

Troilus and Cressida presents a disenchanted version of the Trojan War: The legend and splendor of ancient times are seen in an unfavorable light, as are the chivalric code of the Middle Ages and the theme of courtly love that predominates in Geoffrey Chaucer's *Troilus and Cressida* (c. 1380).

In *All's Well That Ends Well* the heroine, Helena, dedicates herself to the conquest of the young

At the beginning of *Henry VI, Part 1,* the duke of Bedford exclaims: "Hung be the heavens with black, yield day to night! / Comets, importing change of times and states, / Brandish your crystal tresses in the sky / And with them scourge the bad revolting stars / That have consented unto Henry's death!" His words would not have been inappropriate at Elizabeth's funeral.

MEASVRE
For Measure.

Which is the wiser here?
Iustice or Iniquitie?   O thou Cutisse:
O thou Varlet!

Escalus   Elbow

Actus Secundus. Scæna Prima.

Bertram, count of Rousillon, whom she has secretly loved since childhood; but no sooner does he marry her, under the order of the king of France, than he deserts her, and she has to use an elaborate stratagem to win him back.

Measure for Measure is set in Vienna. Duke Vincentio quits his position, leaving his replacement, the puritan Angelo, to enforce an ancient law punishing the crime of fornication with death, to cleanse the city of recent moral corruption. Disguised as a monk, the duke observes the action as the "incorruptible" Angelo falls in love with the young novice Isabella and engages in foul blackmail. Through the ambiguous morality and the obvious allegory of the corruption of power Shakespeare exposes the dark regions of the human conscience.

In *Antony and Cleopatra, Timon of Athens,* and *Coriolanus,* written between 1606 and 1608, Shakespeare goes even further. He returns to the *Parallel Lives* of the Greek biographer Plutarch (c. 46–c. 119) and to the ancient Mediterranean world previously

The plays Shakespeare wrote at the start of James I's reign express doubt, disenchantment, even pessimism. One of the "problem comedies," *Measure for Measure,* shows a distinctly corrupt Viennese society in which the virtue of the cold Isabella is (to us) as unappealing as the vice of the hypocritical Angelo, while the attitude of the duke, who perhaps represents the new sovereign, remains veiled and ambiguous, even as he works behind the scenes for the general good. *Antony and Cleopatra,* however, preserves a sense of lingering fascination and grandeur at the heart of the process of decline, which in the end triumphs and destroys the two main protagonists.

Robert Winter   Christopher Wright   Iohn Wright   Thomas Percy   Guido Fawkes   Robert Catesby   Thomas Winter

Bates

featured in *Titus Andronicus* and *Julius Caesar*, but this time uses Egypt, Athens, and Rome as metaphors for Jacobean society. In these plays one can see reflected the quasi-imperialistic ambitions of James I and the internal problems of an aristocracy that is proud, isolated, split into factions, and incapable of understanding the aspirations of the people. This is the background to the misjudgment that drives a hero like Coriolanus into the arms of Aufidius, Rome's greatest enemy.

Lastly, in the black fable *Timon of Athens* Shakespeare portrays the decline in values and waning power of the nobility that coincided with the rise of

Guy Fawkes and his fellow conspirators (above, in a 1625 print) contrived a plot to blow up the king and Parliament—which is where the procession below is heading. England was deeply disturbed by the Gunpowder Plot, which awakened memories of the killings under Queen Mary. Shakespeare may have known some of the plotters.

entrepreneurs in the worlds of business and finance. Ruined by his friends, to whom he had in his heyday extended the most generous hospitality, Timon retreats to the desert and becomes a misanthropic hermit.

The Sovereign

While he was still James VI of Scotland, James Stuart had pursued scholarly studies and taken an interest in the occult. Author of a number of political treatises and an enlightened lover of the arts, he was renowned for both his intelligence and his interest in witchcraft and the supernatural. In *Daemonologie,* published in 1597, he declared his belief in evil spells and black magic. Once he was king of England, his eccentricities and despotic inclinations led him to shun public occasions and keep to his palaces. His excessive eating and drinking and predilection for beautiful young men, however, quickly created scandal.

The court became known for its ostentation, luxury, extravagance, and love of festivities. A form of spectacle was developed there that remained popular for decades: the masque. This dramatic and musical entertainment was born of a collaboration

between the architect Inigo Jones (1573–1652), who designed the sets, and the playwright and poet Ben Jonson (1572–1637). The first of the genre, *The Masque of Blackness,* was performed at Whitehall Palace on the evening of the Epiphany (January 6) in 1605. It portrayed the introduction to Albion (the ancient literary name for England) of the twelve daughters of Niger, the Ethiopian river god. Moors

Ben Jonson, whose first comedies were put on by Shakespeare's company, increased his reputation in the reign of James I, who commissioned him to write librettos for masques to amuse the court in the winter months. His vast classical knowledge, his reputation as a poet, and his friendship—untouched by rivalry—with Shakespeare, gave him prestige. This portrait (above) is after Abraham van Blyenberch.

Title page (left) of the treatise on demonology by James VI of Scotland, the future James I of England.

and nymphs, Tritons and mermaids, monsters and Nereids rose from the waves, dazzlingly arrayed, to the accompaniment of songs and dances.

The masque was in effect a huge festive show that culminated in a single performance drawing on the skills of technicians and poets and even involving the court in the action. The king, queen, and nobles acted and danced on the stage before concluding the occasion with a ball. In a compliment to the sovereign, the plot was an expression of order and harmony, of which he was represented as the supreme guarantor.

Society and Government

The splendors of the court drew the nobility from the country to London, causing the small communities previously active around the great country houses to fall into decline. The old values came under threat: The traditions of hospitality and duty to the poor slowly disappeared. The gentry were less willing to give board and lodging to the needy in return for light work and shied away from taking in the poor over Christmas and including them in festivities, as had been the custom. The aristocracy of the early 17th century was increasingly reluctant to assume its social responsibilities and little by little left behind the way of life that had characterized the "Merrie England" of Good

B en Jonson produced some thirty masques in collaboration with architect Inigo Jones, who was responsible for the sets and equipment. These sumptuous shows were usually performed only once. The lavish costumes, illustrated in these two watercolors by Inigo Jones, were financed by the nobility or even by the king or queen, who would also take part in the spectacle.

The exquisite wardrobes and sets, the ingenious machinery, and the display of color were matched by the elegant arabesques of the dance steps, which Ben Jonson termed "the hieroglyphics of the court."

Queen Bess (as Elizabeth I was known).

On the political front, James I was eager to unite England and Scotland, and the first seeds of an empire were sown. The Virginia Company of London recruited "volunteers" to colonize the new territories, which courtier and navigator Sir Walter Raleigh had named Virginia in honor of the Virgin Queen. The interest excited at the time by the New World is reflected in *The Tempest,* where Shakespeare dramatizes the conflict between the magus Prospero, would-be exponent of civilization, and the refractory native Caliban.

A New Aesthetic

Exoticism came into fashion, and Shakespeare, like his contemporaries, was delighted to escape for a while from the decadent reality of the realm and to dream. He nevertheless transcended fantasy, using it as a tool to explore the idea of cultural difference.

Until now the unknown world had been seen in fabulous terms; medieval atlases featured a profusion of marvels and strange creatures. Men with the heads of dogs, headless monsters with their eyes and mouths set in their breasts, Sciapodes, whose enormous feet served them as parasols when they lay upside down—all were found side by side with other creatures pronounced real by the famous Greek historian Herodotus (5th century BC).

This legendary vision faded as more of the world was discovered and a more accurate and credible picture developed. While Chaucer, influenced by crosscurrents of English, French,

The Elizabethan period was a great age of travel. Sir Walter Raleigh (opposite, in Nicholas Hilliard's miniature of c. 1585) set foot in Virginia in 1595. He discovered not the anticipated gold but an unknown plant: tobacco. It became a new vice, incurring the censure of the Puritans. In 1608 Captain John Smith explored Chesapeake Bay, shown in this 17th-century map of Virginia (left), and brought back with him an Indian princess, Pocahontas.

and Italian culture, was marked by the medieval vision of the world, the Renaissance writers moved away from it, enthralled instead by the astonishing accounts of travelers to the New World. And with the flowering of Protestantism, England came to perceive of the world as an infinitely varied whole, many-sided and difficult to interpret.

Such ideas run through *Othello* (1604–5), in which Shakespeare daringly makes a Moor the hero of the play. Africans were unknown to the city streets of England and made an appearance only at civic occasions such as the lord mayor's processions in London, where the crowds were both fascinated and disturbed by their

The name of Caliban, the savage slave in *The Tempest*, is a partial anagram of *cannibal*, an identification with the New World, whose imagined grim culinary practices form the subject of this 16th-century engraving (below).

exotic looks. In the popular mind they were linked with the devil's followers or semipagan figures, such as savages. Othello, the noble Moorish general, is the diabolic "other" who stirs fear and simultaneously attracts, both familiar and essentially strange.

It was after this period of great activity—including the marriage of Shakespeare's daughter Susanna to a Stratford doctor in 1607—that Shakespeare's company took over a new playhouse. A new site, new theatrical requirements: Once again the playwright broke new ground.

The Theater at Blackfriars

Blackfriars was an old Dominican priory that had been confiscated in 1538 during the dissolution of the monasteries by Henry VIII. It was situated inside the City walls, at their western extremity, just below Ludgate. This was a liberty extending over about five acres, and, because it escaped the jurisdiction of the City, it was highly popular with those who worked in the theater.

The

ARIEL: Full fathom five thy father lies; / Of his bones are coral made; / Those are pearls that were his eye; / Nothing of him that doth fade / But doth suffer a sea-change / Into something rich and strange" (I, ii).

THE
TEMPEST.

The King's Men began to perform there in 1608. The theater was an indoor hall, rectangular in shape and roughly sixty-five by forty-five feet. It could accommodate an audience of as many as five hundred, all seated, and each paying a relatively high

The Blackfriars auditorium may have resembled these London institutions: Middle Temple (left) and Charterhouse (right).

The Winters Tale.

Winters Tale.

price, which ranged from sixpence to more than two shillings. Between the Globe in the summer and Blackfriars in the winter months, the company was able to perform in all kinds of weather. Furthermore, it became possible to use candles to make the night scenes more realistic. Music was at the same time given a more important role. In the hour leading up to a performance the orchestra would play to welcome the audience, and the intermissions were filled with musical entertainments or masques.

Opposite and above: Modern versions of illustrations from the First Folio edition of *The Tempest* and *The Winter's Tale.*

Most significantly, Shakespeare set out to fully exploit the possibilities offered by the new theater. He transcribed onto the stage a tremendous range of sensation, which combined the spectacular and the fantastic with the deeply moving. The world became a theater, and the theater was the world, dissolving the boundaries between art and life. The stage and the actor became powerful images in themselves.

In his last works, written between 1608 and 1613 —*Pericles, Cymbeline, The Winter's Tale,* and *The Tempest*—Shakespeare returned to comedy. All of these plays culminate in marvelous reunions: miraculous in *Pericles,* where the young Marina rediscovers her father after escaping death at the hands of pirates and in a sordid brothel; moving in *Cymbeline,* where the old man's long-lost sons reappear, having been brought up in a cave in Wales by a faithful soldier; astonishing in *The Winter's Tale,* where Leontes reencounters his daughter Perdita, whom he had banished at birth, believing her to be illegitimate.

This is the baroque world of illusion, which presents life as a dream: "We are such stuff / As dreams are made on, and our little life / Is rounded

with a sleep" are Prospero's words at the end of the masque performed to celebrate the engagement of Ferdinand and Miranda (*The Tempest,* IV, i).

The Globe on Fire

On 29 June 1613, while *Henry VIII* was playing at the Globe, the firing of a blank volley set fire to its thatched roof, and the theater burned to the ground. No one died in the blaze, but it perhaps hastened the playwright's retirement to New Place, in Stratford.

It was there that he wrote *The Two Noble Kinsmen* with John Fletcher, the two men having earlier collaborated—a common practice at the time—on *Henry VIII*. But in this instance it is hard to detect the hand of Shakespeare: The work is distinctly static and heavily melodramatic in its style.

"Retirement" and Private Affairs

All that is known of the last years of Shakespeare's life comes from documents that show that he devoted

Victorian painters were much inspired by Shakespeare's works, in particular his history plays. Here G. H. Harlow portrays Queen Katharine in *Henry VIII* before the ecclesiastical tribunal convoked by the king to consider his application for divorce.

In the purest tradition of 19th-century history painting, the Irish artist Daniel Maclise (1806–70) represents the famous scene in which Hamlet stages "The Murder of Gonzago" before the Danish court (*Hamlet,* III, ii). Hamlet intends that in the course of the play his uncle Claudius will be exposed as the regicide that his father's ghost has proclaimed him to be: "I have heard that guilty creatures sitting at a play / Have by the very cunning of the scene / Been struck so to the soul that presently / They have proclaimed their malefactions. / For murder, though it have no tongue, will speak / With most miraculous organ. I'll have these players / Play something like the murder of my father / Before mine uncle. I'll observe his looks, / I'll tent him to the quick. If 'a do blench / I know my course."

Maclise also made the painting of the banquet scene in *Macbeth* that appears on the following pages.

himself to his private affairs. In 1614 his name was mentioned in a controversy over the enclosure of common land in Stratford in which he had a share. Two years later, on 10 February 1616, his daughter Judith, then more than thirty years old, married Thomas Quiney, a wine merchant and son of an old

friend of Shakespeare's. Evidence suggests the marriage was contracted to cover up a sordid affair of "fornication," which had led to the death of a Margaret Wheeler and her illegitimate child, allegedly fathered by Quiney. It is believed that the scandal may have damaged Shakespeare's health.

On 25 March the playwright summoned his lawyer to alter his will, taking steps to protect Judith from her perhaps unscrupulous husband. In three signed pages Shakespeare left the bulk of his property to his daughter Susanna and his "second best bed" to his wife, Anne, a reference that continues to intrigue biographers. Possibly as a result of a trip to London, from which he returned much weakened, or after an excess of wine over dinner with his friends Michael Drayton and Ben Jonson (according to a story told fifty years later by the vicar of Stratford, John Ward), Shakespeare died on 23 April 1616.

The First Folio: 1623

Two actors in the King's Men, Robert Heminge and Henry Condell, gave the first collected edition of Shakespeare's plays to posterity. The volume, called

the "First Folio"—prepared by printer and publisher William Jaggard and his son Isaac—was published in November 1623. The preliminary pages list thirty-six of his plays (only *Pericles* and *The Two Noble Kinsmen* are omitted), divided into comedies, histories, and tragedies, and also gives the names of the leading men who performed them at the Globe and Blackfriars.

The Final Farewell

Shakespeare's tombstone in Stratford's Holy Trinity Church bears this inscription, said to have been written by him:

> Good friend for Jesus' sake forbear
> To dig the dust enclosed here:
> Blest be the man that spares these stones,
> And curst be he that moves my bones.

A stone bust of Shakespeare at Stratford, carved by Gerard Janssen, shows the playwright with a goose quill in his right hand, a sheet of paper in his left— looking straight ahead with a somewhat empty gaze and an air of satisfaction. But, as Ben Jonson writes in his dedicatory verse for the First Folio, it is the works of his friend William that are the real monument:

> Thou art a Moniment, without a tombe,
> And art alive still, while thy Booke doth live.

S hakespeare signed all three pages of the will drawn up for him by Warwick lawyer Francis Collins. These three signatures are rare instances of his authenticated handwriting.

S hakespeare's monument in a Stratford church (opposite).

" Fear no more the heat o' th' sun / Nor the furious winter's rages; / Thou thy worldly task hast done, / Home art gone, and ta'en thy wages. / Golden lads and girls all must, / As chimney-sweepers, come to dust. "
Cymbeline (I, ii)

B elow and p. 128: Pages from the First Folio, 1623.

The Workes of William Shakespeare,
containing all his Comedies, Histories, and
Tragedies: Truely set forth, according to their first
ORIGINALL.

The Names of the Principall Actors
in all these Playes.

William Shakespeare.	Samuel Gilburne.
Richard Burbadge.	Robert Armin.
John Hemmings.	William Ostler.
Augustine Phillips.	Nathan Field.
William Kempt.	John Underwood.
Thomas Poope.	Nicholas Tooley.
George Bryan.	William Ecclestone.
Henry Condell.	Joseph Taylor.
William Slye.	Robert Benfield.
Richard Cowly.	Robert Goughe.
John Lowine.	Richard Robinson.
Samuell Crosse.	John Shancke.
Alexander Cooke.	John Rice.

A CATALOGVE

of the feuerall Comedies, Histories, and Tragedies contained in this Volume.

DOCUMENTS

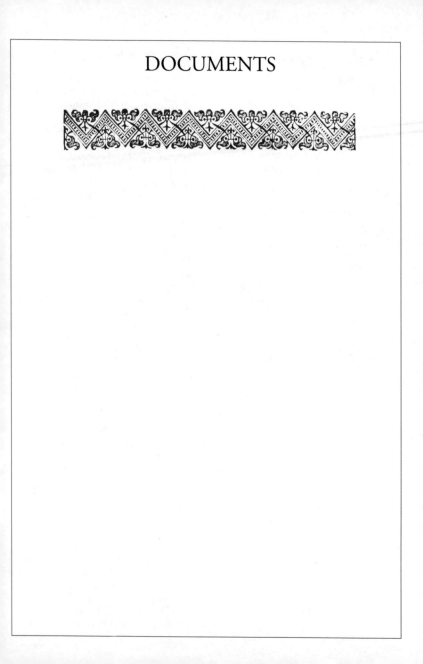

Shakespeare the Man

The documentary evidence of Shakespeare's personal life is meager, but not more so than that of most people of his time and rank. His baptism and burial are entered in the register of the Stratford parish church, as are the baptisms of his children. Another important existing document is Shakespeare's marriage license, which had to be specially authorized by the bishop of Worcester.

Shakespeare and the Law

There are a number of legal documents relating to various aspects of Shakespeare's life. They pertain to his shares in the Globe Theatre company, his tax problems, his application for a coat of arms, and his purchase of property in London and Stratford. Of these documents, the one that sheds the most light on his personality was discovered in 1909.

In 1604 Shakespeare was lodging in the house of a family called Mountjoy, on Silver Street in London. Christopher Mountjoy was a French maker of wigs and ornamental headgear. One of his apprentices was a man named Stephen Belott, who in November 1604 married his master's daughter Mary. Eight years later a dispute arose over how much Mountjoy had promised to give Belott as a dowry for his daughter. The following testimonies are from a transcription of the court hearings that were held to resolve the dispute. The entire transcription of the Belott-Mountjoy case can be read in the Public Record Office in London.

Mr William Shakespeare tould him… that the defendant sent him, the said Mr Shakespeare, to the plaintiff about suche a marriadge to be hadd betweene them, and Shakespeare tould this deponent that the defendant tould him that yf the plaintiff would marrye the said Marye his daughter he would geve him the plaintiff a some of monney with her for a porcion in marriadge with her. And that yf he the plaintiff did not marry with her, the said Marye, and shee with the plaintiff shee should never coste him, the defendant her ffather, a groat. Whereuppon, and in regard Mr Shakespeare hadd tould them that they should have a some of monney for a porcion from the father, they weare made suer by Mr Shakespeare by geuinge there consent, and agreed to marrye,…and did marrye.

Another witness stated:

…that the plaintiff did requeste…him to goe with his wyffe to Shakespe[are] to understande the truthe howe muche and what the defendant did promise [to] bestowe on his daughter in marriadge with him the plaintiff, who did soe. And askinge Shakespeare therof, he answered that he promissed yf the plaintiff would marrye with Marye his the defendantes onlye daughter, he the defendant would by his promise as he remembered geve the plaintiff with her in marriadge about the some of ffyftye poundes in money and certayne houshould stuffe.

Shakespeare was accordingly called from Stratford to testify, which he did on 11 May 1612. Not surprisingly after so long an interval, he could not remember what had been promised. What is interesting for us is that this is a unique glimpse of Shakespeare in a domestic setting (interesting, too, that he seems not to know his exact age).

William Shakespeare of Stratford upon Aven in the Countye of Warwicke gentleman of the age of xlviij yeres or thereaboutes sworne and examined the daye and yere abovesaid deposethe & sayethe

To the first interrogatory this deponent sayethe he knowethe the partyes plaintiff and deffendant and hathe know[ne] them bothe as he now remembrethe for the space of tenne yeres or thereaboutes.

To the second interrogatory this deponent sayeth he did know the complainant when he was servant with the deffendant, and that duringe the tyme of his the complainantes service with the said deffendant he the said complainant to this deponentes knowledge did well and honestly behave himselfe, but to this deponentes remembrance he hath not heard the deffendant confesse that he had gott any great profitt and comodytye by the service of the said complainant, but this deponent saithe he verely thinkethe that the said complainant was a very good and industrious servant in the said service. And more he canott depose to the said interrogatory.

To the third interrogatory this deponent sayethe that it did evydentlye appeare that the said deffendant did all the tyme of the said complainantes service with him beare and shew great good will and affeccion towardes the said complainant, and that he hath hard the deffendant and his wyefe diverse and sundry tymes saye and reporte that the said complainant was a very honest fellow: And this deponent sayethe that the said deffendant did make a mocion unto the complainant of marriadge with the said Mary in the bill mencioned beinge the said deffendantes sole chyld and daughter, and willinglye offered to performe the same yf the said complainant shold seeme to be content and well like thereof: And further this deponent sayethe that the said deffendantes wyeffe did sollicitt and entreat this deponent to move and perswade the said complainant to effect the said marriadge, and accordingly this deponent did move and perswade the complainant therunto: And more to this interrogatorye he cannott depose.

To the ffourth interrogatory this deponent sayth that the defendant promissed to geve the said complainant a porcion…in marriadg[e] with Marye his daughter, but what certayne… porcion he rememberethe not, nor when to be payed…, nor knoweth that the defendant promissed the… plaintiff twoe hundered poundes with his daughter Marye at the tyme of his decease. But sayth that the plaintiff was dwellinge with the defendant in his house, and they had amongeste them selves manye conferences about there marriadge which afterwarde was consumated and solempnized. And more he cannott depose.

To the vth interrogatory this deponent sayth he can saye nothinge touchinge any parte or poynte of the same interrogatory, for he knoweth not what implementes and necessaries of houshould stuffe the defendant gave the plaintiff in marriadge with his daughter Marye.

Willm Shakp

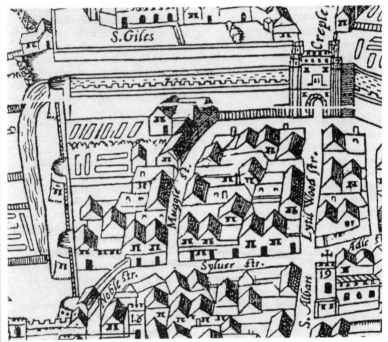

Detail of a London map of the 1550s showing Silver Street, where in 1604 Shakespeare lodged with the family of a wig maker named Mountjoy. A character in one of Ben Jonson's plays says of another, "All her teeth were made in the Blackfriars, both her eyebrows in the Strand, and her hair in Silver Street."

Shakespeare the Lender

*No letters from Shakespeare survive, but
there is one to him from a Stratford
neighbor, Richard Quiney, dated
25 October 1598, asking for a loan.
Eighteen years later, in February 1616,
Richard Quiney's son, Thomas, married
Shakespeare's daughter Judith.*

To my Loveinge good ffrend &
contreymann Mr Wm. Shackespere
deliver thees.

Loveinge Contreyman, I am bolde of
yowe as of a ffrende, craveinge yowre
helpe with xxx*ll* uppon Mr Bushells &
my securytee or Mr Myttons with me.
Mr Rosswell is nott come to London as
yeate & I have especiall cawse. Yowe
shall ffrende me muche in helpeinge
me out of all the debettes I owe in
London, I thancke god, & muche quiet
my mynde which wolde nott be
indebeted. I am nowe towardes the
Cowrte in hope of answer for the
dispatche of my Buysenes. Yowe shall
neither loase creddytt nor monney by
me, the Lorde wyllinge, & nowe butt
perswade yowre selfe soe as I hope &
yowe shall nott need to feare butt with
all hartie thanckefullenes I will holde
my tyme & content yowre ffrende, &
yf we Bargaine farther yowe shalbe the
paiemaster yowre self. My tyme biddes
me hasten to an ende & soe I committ
thys [to] yowre care & hope of yowre
helpe. I feare I shall nott be backe thys
night ffrom the Cowrte. Haste. The
Lorde be with yowe & with us all
Amen. ffrom the Bell [Inn] in Carter
Lane the 25 October 1598. Yowres in
all kyndenes Ryc. Quyney.

Letter at the Shakespeare
Birthplace Trust, Stratford

Shakespeare's Will

*By far the longest and most informative
of the legal documents to have survived is
Shakespeare's will, which was drawn up
in January 1616 and amended in
March. It tells us much about his circumstances and the people closest to him but
sometimes raises more questions than it
answers—most notably the bequest to his
wife, Anne, of his "second best bed."*

In the name of God, amen! I William
Shackspeare, of Stratford upon Avon in
the countie of Warr. gent., in perfect
health and memorie, God be praysed,
doe make and ordayne this my last will
and testament in manner and forme
followeing, that ys to saye, First, I
comend my soule into the handes of
God my Creator, hoping and assuredlie
beleeving, through thonelie merittes of
Jesus Christe my Saviour, to be made
partaker of lyfe everlastinge, and my
bodye to the earth whereof yt ys made.

Item, I gyve and bequeath unto my
daughter Judyth one hundred and
fyftie poundes of lawfull English
money, to be paied unto her in manner
and forme followeing, that ys to saye,
one hundred poundes in discharge of
her marriage porcion within one yeare
after my deceas....

Item, I gyve and bequeath unto my
saied daughter Judith one hundred and
fyftie poundes more, if shee or anie
issue of her bodie be lyvinge att thend
of three yeares next ensueing the daie
of the date of this my will....

Item, I gyve and bequeath unto my
saied sister Jone xx.li. and all my
wearing apparrell, to be paied and
delivered within one yeare after my
deceas; and I doe will and devise unto
her the house with thappurtenaunces in

Stratford, wherein she dwelleth, for her naturall lief, under the yearelie rent of xij.d. Item, I gyve and bequeath unto her three sonns, William Harte,... Hart, and Michaell Harte, fyve poundes a peece, to be payed within one yeare after my deceas....

Item, I gyve and bequeath unto the poore of Stratford aforesaied tenn poundes; to Mr. Thomas Combe my sword; to Thomas Russell esquier fyve poundes, and to Frauncis Collins of the borough of Warr. in the countie of Warr. gent. thirteene poundes, sixe shillinges, and eight pence, to be paied within one yeare after my deceas. Item, I gyve and bequeath to Mr. Richard Tyler thelder Hamlett Sadler xxvj.s. viij.d. to buy him a ringe; to William Raynoldes, gent., xxvj.s. viij.d. to buy him a ringe;... to my god-son William Walker xx.s. in gold; to Anthonye Nashe gent. xxvj.s. viij.d., and to Mr. John Nashe xxvj.s. viij.d. in gold; and to my fellowes, John Hemynges, Richard Burbage, and Henry Cundell, xxvj.s. viij.d. a peece to buy them ringes.

Item, I gyve, will, bequeath and devise, unto my daughter Susanna Hall, for better enabling of her to performe this my will, and towardes the performans thereof, all that capitall messuage or tenemente, with thappurtenaunces, in Stratford aforesaied, called the Newe Place, wherein I nowe dwell, and twoe messuages or tenementes with thappurtenaunces, scituat lyeing and being in Henley streete within the borough of Stratford aforesaied; and all my barnes, stables, orchardes, gardens, landes, tenementes and hereditamentes whatsoever, scituat lyeing and being, or to be had, receyved, perceyved, or taken, within the townes, hamlettes, villages, fieldes and groundes of Stratford-upon-Avon, Oldstratford, Bushopton, and Welcombe, or in anie of them in the saied countie of Warr. And alsoe all that messuage or tenemente with thappurtenaunces wherein one John Robinson dwelleth, scituat lyeing and being in the Blackfriers in London nere the Wardrobe; and all other my landes, tenementes, and hereditamentes whatsoever, To have and to hold all and singuler the saied premisses with their appurtenaunces unto the saied Susanna Hall for and during the terme of her naturall lief....

Item, I gyve unto my wiefe my second best bed with the furniture. Item, I gyve and bequeath to my saied daughter Judith my broad silver gilt bole. All the rest of my goodes, chattels, leases, plate, jewels, and household stuffe whatsoever, after my dettes and legasies paied, and my funerall expences discharged, I gyve, devise, and bequeath to my sonne in lawe, John Hall gent., and my daughter Susanna, his wief, whom I ordaine and make executours of this my last will and testament. And I doe intreat and appoint the saied Thomas Russell esquier and Frauncis Collins gent. to be overseers hereof, and doe revoke all former wills, and publishe this to be my last will and testament. In witnes whereof I have hereunto put my hand the daie and yeare first above written.—By me, William Shakespeare.

Witnes to the publishing hereof, —Fra: Collyns; Julius Shawe; John Robinson; Hamnet Sadler; Robert Whattcott.

Will preserved in the Public Record Office, London

The last page of Shakespeare's will, with the witnesses' names at the bottom. The will was drawn up by a lawyer. Only the words "By me, William Shakespeare" are in his own handwriting.

Theaters and Theatergoing

Although a visit to a London theater was one of the expeditions that every interested visitor tried to make, there are few surviving firsthand accounts, and those few are tantalizingly vague.

Dutchman Johannes de Witt, who in 1596 made a sketch of the Swan Theatre (see p. 68), had this to say about it:

There are four amphitheatres in London of notable beauty, which from their diverse signs bear diverse names. In each of them a different play is daily exhibited to the populace. The two more magnificent of these are situated to the southward beyond the Thames, and from the signs suspended before them are called the Rose and the Swan. The two others are outside the city towards the north on the highway which issues through the Episcopal Gate, called in the vernacular Bishopgate. There is also a fifth [the Bear Garden], but of dissimilar structure, devoted to the baiting of beasts, where are maintained in separate cages and enclosures many bears and dogs of stupendous size, which are kept for fighting, furnishing thereby a most delightful spectacle to men. Of all the theatres, however, the largest and the most magnificent is that one of which the sign is a swan, called in the vernacular the Swan Theatre; for it accommodates in its seats three thousand persons, and is built of a mass of flint stones (of which there is a prodigious supply in Britain), and supported by wooden columns painted in such excellent imitation of marble that it is able to deceive even the most cunning. Since its form resembles that of a Roman work, I have made a sketch of it above.

In 1599 a visitor from Basel named Thomas Platter saw Julius Caesar.

After dinner on the 21st of September, at about two o'clock, I went with my companions over the water, and in the strewn roof-house saw the tragedy of the first Emperor Julius with at least fifteen characters very well acted. At the end of the comedy they danced according to their custom with extreme elegance. Two in men's clothes and two in women's gave this peformance, in wonderful combination with each other. On another occasion, I also saw after dinner a comedy, not far from our inn, in the suburb; if I remember right, in Bishopsgate. Here they represented various nations, with whom on each occasion an Englishman fought for his daughter, and overcame them all except the German, who won the daughter in fight. He then sat down with him, and gave him and his servant strong drink, so that they both got drunk, and the servant threw his shoe at his master's head and they both fell asleep. Meanwhile the Englishman went into the tent, robbed the German of his gains, and thus he outwitted the German also. At the end they danced very elegantly both in English and in Irish fashion. And thus every day at two o'clock in the afternoon in the city of London two and sometimes three comedies are performed, at separate places, wherewith folk make merry together, and whichever does best gets the greatest audience. The places are so built, that they play on a raised platform, and every one can well see it all. There are, however, separate galleries and there one stands more comfortably and moreover can sit, but one pays more for it. Thus anyone who remains on the level standing pays only one English penny: but if he wants to sit, he is let in at a further door, and there he gives another penny. If he desires to sit on a cushion in the most comfortable place of all, where he not

only sees everything well, but can also be seen, then he gives yet another English penny at another door. And in the pauses of the comedy food and drink are carried round amongst the people, and one can thus refresh himself at his own cost.

The comedians are most expensively and elegantly apparelled, since it is customary in England, when distinguished gentlemen or knights die, for nearly the finest of their clothes to be made over and given to their servants, and as it is not proper for them to wear such clothes but only to imitate them, they give them to the comedians to purchase for a small sum.

What they can thus produce daily by way of mirth in the comedies, every one knows well, who has happened to see them acting or playing....

With such and many other pastimes besides the English spend their time; in the comedies they learn what is going on in other lands, and this happens without alarm, husband and wife together in a familiar place, since for the most part the English do not much use to travel, but are content ever to learn of foreign matters at home, and ever to take their pastime.

On 29 June 1613 the Globe Theatre burned down during a performance of Henry VIII. The Survey of London *by John Stow (originally published in 1598, but updated by Edmond Howes after Stow's death in 1605) gives this account:*

Upon S. Peters day last, the play-house or Theater, called the Globe, upon the Banck-side near London, by negligent discharging of a peal of ordinance, close to the south-side thereof, the thatch took fire, and the wind sodainly disperst the flame round about, and in a very short space the whole building was quite consumed, and no man hurt; the house being filled with people to behold the play, viz. of Henry the Eighth. And the next spring it was new builded in far fairer manner than before.

A letter from Sir Henry Wotton (1568–1639) to his nephew goes into more detail.

Now to let matters of state sleep, I will entertain you at the present with what has happened this week at the Bank's side. The King's players had a new play, called *All is True,* representing some principal pieces of the reign of Henry VIII, which was set forth with many extraordinary circumstances of pomp and majesty, even to the matting of the stage; the Knights of the Order with their Georges and garters, the Guards with their embroidered coats, and the like: sufficient in truth within a while to make greatness very familiar, if not ridiculous. Now, King Henry making a masque at the Cardinal Wolsey's house, and certain chambers being shot off at his entry, some of the paper, or other stuff, wherewith one of them was stopped, did light on the thatch, where being thought at first but an idle smoke, and their eyes more attentive to the show, it kindled inwardly, and ran round like a train, consuming within less than an hour the whole house to the very grounds. This was the fatal period of that virtuous fabric, wherein yet nothing did perish but wood and straw, and a few forsaken cloaks; only one man had his breeches set on fire, that would perhaps have broiled him, if he had not by the benefit of a provident wit put it out with bottle ale.

Letter of 1 July 1613

The Rose Theatre

Until recently no vestige of an Elizabethan theater was thought to exist. But in 1988 workers excavating for a new office complex near Southwark Bridge came upon the foundation of the Rose Theatre. Built about 1587, the Rose was owned and managed by Burbage's rival, Philip Henslowe, and it is therefore unlikely that any of Shakespeare's plays were performed there (except possibly Henry VI*). The physical remains are nevertheless of outstanding value in providing information about the size, shape, and planning of an Elizabethan playhouse.*

It was an irregular polygon with the entrance on the south side and the stage on the north. The gap between the inner and outer walls gives the width of the galleries (almost twelve feet). The central space sloped down to the stage—a fact hitherto unsuspected by theater historians. The stage area itself was fragmentary but gave evidence of having been enlarged by being extended backward, a development confirmed by Henslowe's accounts for 1592.

The site has been carefully preserved but is immured in the basement of the office complex.

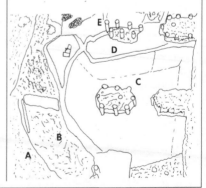

The foundation of the Rose Theatre, as it was revealed in 1988. (The two large concrete slabs and the posts at the top of the picture belong to modern buildings and should be ignored.) The main features (see key opposite) are (A) the outer wall; (B) the inner wall of the gallery; (C) the standing space for spectators; (D) the original position of the stage; and (E) the later position of the stage after the theater was extended to the north (top).

Shakespeare the Author

The First Folio, published in 1623, divided Shakespeare's plays into histories, comedies, and tragedies. The comedies fall into four distinct categories: the early comedies, the romantic comedies, the problem comedies, and those of the last period, termed "romances" or tragi-comedies. Scholars also distinguish among the tragedies. There are the Roman tragedies, namely Julius Caesar, Antony and Cleopatra, *and* Coriolanus; *the tragedies of passion, such as* Romeo and Juliet *and* Othello; *the revenge tragedies,* Titus Andronicus *and* Hamlet; *and finally those based on historical chronicles,* King Lear *and* Macbeth.

The Diversity of Shakespeare's Plays

With the exception of two isolated works, *King John* (1596–7) and *Henry VIII* (1612–3), the history plays consist essentially of two tetralogies, which form a sequence of eight plays. In the First Folio they are presented in historical chronological order rather than in order of composition.

The subject matter of the histories is drawn from the chronicles of British historians John Hall and Raphael Holinshed. The plays illustrate the vicissitudes of Fortune—whose fickle wheel casts princes into the depths after raising them to the heights—and also the diverse manifestations of divine providence.

These works portray the destiny of kings, a destiny often unhappy or tragic. The crown, an object of fascination, seems to crush its wearer, who is forced to confront treachery, masked by flattery, or open rebellion. The sovereign, despite his aura of divine legitimacy, lives under threat of usurpation. He must wield his authority to kill any stirrings of rebellion in their infancy. In some instances the king proves incompetent, or his right to rule is challenged—as in the case of Richard II, blinded by parasitic councillors, favorites who destroy the garden symbolic of his kingdom—while in others he is a villain, or a monster, on the lines of Richard III, who inflicts an age of bloody tyranny on his people. The series of plays about history and royal reigns illustrates the theme of the monarch's grandeur and destitution: Stripped of the trappings and symbols of his power, he is revealed as a man like any other, weak and full of anguish in the face of death. These histories, in which politics are as much an expression of rivalries between families and clans as of human ambition and hubris, resound with the clash of battle and are rendered on the stage as terrible martial displays disintegrating into breathless combat.

The comedies are an important part of Shakespeare's work; he wrote them throughout his career, and they account for half of his plays. The first comedies were written between the years 1593 and 1596 and consist of five main titles: *The Comedy of Errors, The Taming of the Shrew, The Two Gentlemen of Verona, Love's Labour's Lost,* and *A Midsummer Night's Dream.* These plays are all very different from each other and present different types of humor in their handling of the themes of illusion and mistaken identity, as well as rivalry in love and the war between the sexes.

The comedies of the mature period, also known as the romantic comedies, were all written in the five following years, between 1596 and 1600, and include *The Merchant of Venice, Much Ado About Nothing, As You Like It,* and *Twelfth Night. The Merry Wives of Windsor,* in a category apart, was written in two or three weeks in 1599 or 1600 in response to the queen's wish to see Falstaff in a romantic intrigue.

In the romantic comedies it is love that forms the principal theme; love is the primary concern of the young protagonists, whose impulses are thwarted by parental opposition or the intrigues of mean-minded individuals. However, after a period of trials that takes them into a strange and, at the same time, restorative environment (the forest near Athens in *A Midsummer Night's Dream,* Portia's palace at Belmont in *The Merchant of Venice*), the pains of love are brought to an end, resolved by a wedding feast or multiple marriages.

Shakespeare then wrote the darker comedies, known as the problem comedies because of their more philosophical tone or comparatively disturbing character; for example, *Troilus and Cressida,* a play sometimes classed among the tragedies, *All's Well That Ends Well,* and *Measure for Measure.*

Strangely, Shakespeare wrote only a few tragedies at the beginning of his career. Three years after *Titus Andronicus,* a play inspired by Seneca and the mythology of Ovid—and once thought to be impossible to stage because of its multiple atrocities and scenes of mutilation and cannibalism—he wrote *Romeo and Juliet.* This is a tragedy of passion, but even more of fate, for the death of the young couple is brought about by a series of unhappy coincidences rather than by evil or malevolent characters; until the very end one hopes that the fatal outcome will be avoided. The play is further identified as an early work by its stirring lyricism, the intensity of the images, and the pronounced contrasts between night and day, youth and age, love and death.

Easier to categorize are the Roman tragedies, *Julius Caesar, Antony and Cleopatra,* and *Coriolanus,* which follow in the footsteps of the historical plays of the first period. This time Shakespeare finds his sources in 1st-century biographer Plutarch's *Parallel Lives,* translated in 1579 by Thomas North, rather than in Holinshed's *Chronicles. Julius Caesar* and *Coriolanus* are as much political dramas as cruel confrontations between the envisioned ideal (Brutus) or ambition (Coriolanus) and reality; *Antony and Cleopatra* is first and foremost a tragedy of sexual passion.

But it is above all the four great tragedies, *Hamlet, Othello, King Lear,* and *Macbeth,* that characterize the second period of Shakespeare's career, which began when his troupe moved to the Globe Theatre. *Hamlet* is in the genre of the revenge tragedy originated by Thomas Kyd in *The Spanish Tragedy* (1592) and probably also in another, now lost, pre-*Hamlet* play which would have served Shakespeare as a model. However, *Hamlet* is also a problem play, its hero questioning himself as to the reality of his father's ghost and, unlike other avengers, procrastinating in the execution of the task with which the specter has charged him. A political tragedy, a philosophical drama, a contemplation on theater by the theater (in the scenes featuring actors and in the play within the play), this tragedy is Shakespeare's best known, and in its richness and complexity it holds a central place in his work.

Othello is a domestic tragedy, a tragedy of illusion, in which the relation-ship between appearance and reality is distorted by the cunning of an evil manipulator and the credulity of a foreigner who believes in the power of words.

King Lear, the plot of which is drawn from English historical legend, is also a tale of illusion, of the blindness of a king mistreated by two of his daughters, who flatter him with fine words. Lear makes the mistake of dividing his kingdom between them while banishing the third daughter; she loves him most but refuses to take part in the masquerade of declarations of affection demanded by the old king. It takes the trials of madness, destitution, confrontation with the fool and with Edgar, disguised as a beggar and also banished by his own father, to bring Lear to the point of understanding the frailty of the human condition and the enormity of his own error.

Macbeth marks a forceful return to the supernatural, glimpsed in the ghostly apparitions of *Hamlet,* with the incantations and machinations of the three Weird Sisters, who come to tempt the valiant warrior in the wake of battle and sow doubt and ambition in his mind. Driven to regicide by his wife's greed for power, he becomes a bloody tyrant, ready to make every compromise with the forces of evil to preserve his power. A metaphysical drama as much as a political tragedy, *Macbeth* translates the conflict of good and evil into cosmic terms and, in the power of its language, provides a terrifying vision of the empire of darkness and its business of destroying innocence and the springs of life.

In the last stage of his career Shakespeare concentrated on a relatively new type of play known as a romance, no doubt written to satisfy the public taste for sentiment and to exploit the marvelous stage effects made possible by the acquisition of the private indoor theater at Blackfriars. These are the works written between 1608 and 1613, namely *Pericles, Cymbeline, The Winter's Tale, The Tempest,* and *The Two Noble Kinsmen,* leaving aside the play *Henry VIII,* which is closer in style to the historical dramas than to the last comedies.

François Laroque

The Mystery of "Mr. W. H."

Shakespeare's sonnets were published in 1609, though not by him. Most of them had been written ten or even twenty years earlier. The first 127 are addressed to a beautiful young man whom the poet urges to marry and beget a child. Another 27 concern a "dark lady" who is the poet's mistress. In lieu of a dedication, the following enigmatic note appears on the first page. Although clearly not written by Shakespeare ("T. T." is the printer, Thomas Thorpe), it has given rise to more speculation than anything he ever wrote. Who is "Mr. W. H."? The once favorite candidate was Shakespeare's patron Henry Wriothesley ("H. W."); there have been many other suggestions and will doubtless be many more.

TO . THE . ONLIE . BEGET TER . OF.
THESE . INSVING . SONNETS.
Mr. W. H. ALL . HAPPINESSE.
AND . THAT . ETERNITIE.
PROMISED.

BY.

OVR . EVER-LIVING . POET.

WISHETH.

THE . WELL-WISHING.
ADVENTVRER . IN.
SETTING.
FORTH.

T. T.

The enigmatic dedication to Shakespeare's *Sonnets*, 1609.

The Early Works

Shakespeare was a poet before he was a playwright. Venus and Adonis *was published in 1593,* The Rape of Lucrece *in 1594. These poems are the only works that Shakespeare seems to have published himself. Both contain effusive dedications to Henry Wriothesley, earl of Southampton, to whom the young poet was clearly looking as a patron.*

These dedications are the only surviving written statements we have by Shakespeare on any of his works. How close the relationship was, or what benefits Wriothesley's patronage brought the playwright, is unknown (a later story relating that he loaned Shakespeare £1000 seems unlikely). Below is the dedication to Venus and Adonis.

Right Honourable

I know not how I shall offend in dedicating my unpolished lines to your lordship, nor how the world will censure me for choosing so strong a prop to support so weak a burden: only, if your honour seem but pleased, I account myself highly praised, and vow to take advantage of all idle hours, till I have honoured you with some graver labour. But if the first heir of my invention prove deformed, I shall be sorry it had so noble a godfather, and never after ear so barren a land, for fear it yield me still so bad a harvest. I leave it to your honourable survey, and your honour to your heart's content; which I wish may always answer your own wish, and the world's hopeful expectation.

Your honour's in all duty,
William Shakespeare

TO THE RIGHT

HONOVRABLE, HENRY
VVriothefley, Earle of Southhampton,
and Baron of Titchfield.

HE loue I dedicate to your Lordſhip is without end: wherof this Pamphlet without beginning is but a ſuperfluous Moity. The warrant I haue of your Honourable diſpoſition, not the worth of my vntutord Lines makes it aſſured of acceptance. VVhat I haue done is yours, what I haue to doe is yours, being part in all I haue, deuoted yours. VVere my worth greater, my duety would ſhew greater, meane time, as it is, it is bound to your Lordſhip; To whom I wiſh long life ſtill lengthned with all happineſſe.

Your Lordſhips in all duety,

William Shakeſpeare.

D edication page of *The Rape of Lucrece,*
1594.

A Shakespeare Manuscript?

Around 1592–3 the playwrights Anthony Munday and Henry Chettle produced the script of a play called Sir Thomas More *and submitted it to the queen's master of revels, Edmund Tilney, whose job it was to license plays for public performance.* Sir Thomas More contained a number of problems, one of which was a scene showing Londoners rioting against foreign merchants in the City and being pacified by the statesman More (an incident that actually occurred in 1517). Tilney was nervous because a new wave of xenophobic feeling was at that time disturbing the City. He wrote: "Leave out the insurrection wholly, with the cause thereof, and begin with Sir Thomas More at the Mayor's sessions —with a report afterwards of his good service done being Sheriff of London upon a mutiny against the Lombards —only by a short report and not

otherwise—at your own perils. E. Tilney."

This would have meant virtually sabotaging the play, and what seems to have happened is that Munday and Chettle called on the services of another playwright, who rewrote the whole scene, providing More with a powerful speech recommending law and order. Even this, however, failed to win approval from Tilney. It was never acted or printed, and the manuscript was left to molder, eventually finding its way into the collection of the British Library, London.

It is in a chaotic and sometimes illegible state, in at least five different handwritings, but what has attracted the interest of scholars is the three pages containing the revised scene of More and the rioters. They are written in a different hand from the rest, and the style is in many obvious ways superior. Was Shakespeare the author, and do we have here a unique example of a manuscript in his own hand? The arguments— based on style, content, spelling, and handwriting—are strong, but the final answer can never be known.

The content of More's speech, arguing for peace, compromise, and submission to lawful authority, is in tune with similar speeches in Shakespeare's works; the style is direct but rich in imagery; and even the spelling accords with what is known (or can be deduced) of Shakespeare's spelling—most notably "scilens" for "silence." The question will no doubt always remain open, except in the unlikely event that another manuscript turns up. In the extract printed here More argues with the crowd, appealing to their sense of justice and asking them to put themselves in the place of the foreigners whom they want to drive out. He promises mercy from the king, but in reality, that promise was not kept.

Part of the 1592–3 manuscript of *Sir Thomas More* (above), with the same passage in modern English (below).

MORE: To any German province, Spain or Portugal,
Nay, anywhere that not adheres to England
Why, you must needs be strangers. Would you be pleased
To find a nation of such barbarous temper,
That, breaking out in hideous violence,
Would not afford you an abode on earth,
Whet their detested knives against your throats,
Spurn you like dogs and like as if that God
Owed not nor made not you, nor that the elements
Were not all appropriate to your comforts
But chartered unto them? What would you think
To be thus used? This is the strangers' case,
And this your montanish inhumanity.

ALL: Faith! He says true; let's do as we may be done by.

LINCOLN: We'll be ruled by you, Master More, if you'll stand our friend to procure our pardon.

MORE: Submit you to these noble gentlemen,
Entreat their mediation to the King,
Give up yourself to form, obey the Magistrate,
And there's no doubt but mercy may be found
If you so seek it.

Public Opinion

The first public mention of Shakespeare as a playwright is a hostile one. In Robert Greene's Groatsworth of Wit Bought with a Million of Repentance *of 1592, Greene warns three other dramatists (Christopher Marlowe and probably George Peele and Thomas Nashe) against an ignorant newcomer, not educated at a university, who is shouldering his way into the profession.*

Base minded men al three of you, if by my miserie ye be not warned; for unto none of you, like me, sought those burres to cleave; those puppits, I meane, that speake from our mouths, those anticks garnish in our colours. Is it not strange that I, to whom they al have beene beholding, is it not like that you to whome they all have beene beholding, shall, were ye in that case that I am now, be both at once of them forsaken? Yes, trust them not; for there is an upstart crow, beautified with our feathers, that, with his *Tygers heart wrapt in a Players hide*, supposes he is as well able to bumbast out a blanke verse as the best of you; and being an absolute *Johannes Factotum*, is in his owne conceit the onely Shake-scene in a countrie.

O that I might intreate your rare wits to be imployed in more profitable courses, and let those apes imitate your past excellence, and never more acquaint them with your admired inventions! I know the best husband of you all will never prove an usurer, and the kindest of them all wil never proove a kinde nurse; yet, whilst you may, seeke you better maisters; for it is pittie men of such rare wits should be subject to the pleasures of such rude groomes.

More interesting than this mean-spirited attack by the dying Greene is the response that it provoked from another author, Henry Chettle (c. 1560–1607). In the preface to Kind-Hart's Dream *(1592) he tells us that two people had taken offense at Greene's words. One of them was probably Marlowe, whom Greene had called an atheist and a disciple of Machiavelli; the other was clearly Shakespeare. The first, says Chettle, he cares not if he never meets; the second had previously been unknown to him, but upon looking into the matter he feels obliged to apologize.*

About three moneths since died M. Robert Greene, leaving many papers in sundry booksellers hands, among other his Groatsworth of Wit, in which a letter, written to divers play-makers, is offensively by one or two of them taken; and because on the dead they cannot be avenged, they wilfully forge in their conceites a living author; and after tossing it two and fro, no remedy but it must light on me. How I have all the time of my conversing in printing hindred the bitter inveying against schollers, it hath been very well knowne; and how in that I dealt, I can sufficiently proove. With neither of them that take offence was I acquainted, and with one of them I care not if I never be. The other, whome at that time I did not so much spare as since I wish I had, for that, as I have moderated the heate of living writers, and might have usde my owne discretion,—especially in such a case, the author beeing dead,—that I did not I am as sory as if the originall fault had beene my fault, because myselfe have seene his demeanor no lesse civill, than he exelent in the qualitie he professes;—besides, divers of worship have reported his uprightnes of dealing, which argues his honesty, and his facetious grace in writting, that aprooves his art.

This is a curious incident. Shakespeare evidently had powerful friends to protest on his behalf. Who were they? A book by a scholarly clergyman named Francis Meres, Palladis Tamia: Wits Treasury (1598), contains a "comparative discourse of our English Poets with the Greek, Latin and Italian poets," in the course of which are listed what were evidently regarded as Shakespeare's best plays up to that time.

As Plautus and Seneca are accounted the best for comedy and tragedy among the Latines, so Shakespeare among the English is the most excellent in both kinds for the stage; for comedy, witnes his Gentlemen of Verona, his Errors, his Love labors lost, his Love labours wonne, his Midsummers night dreame, and his Merchant of Venice; for tragedy, his Richard the 2, Richard the 3, Henry the 4, King John, Titus Andronicus and his Romeo and Juliet. As Epius Stolo said that the Muses would speake with Plautus tongue, if they would speak Latin; so I say that the Muses would speak with Shakespeare's fine filed phrase, if they would speake English.

Friends and Foes

When John Heminge and Henry Condell collected Shakespeare's plays to be published in the First Folio of 1623, they added their tribute to him and to the ease with which he wrote.

It had bene a thing, we confesse, worthie to have bene wished, that the Author himselfe had liv'd to have set forth, and overseen his owne writings; But since it hath been ordain'd otherwise, and he by death departed from that right, we pray you do not envie his Friends, the office of their care, and paine, to have collected & publish'd them, and so to have publish'd them, as where (before) you were abus'd with diverse stolne, and surreptitious copies, maimed, and deformed by the frauds and stealthes of iniurious impostors, that expos'd them: even those, are now offer'd to your view cur'd, and perfect of their limbes; and all the rest, absolute in their numbers, as he conceived them. Who, as he was a happie imitator of Nature, was a most gentle expresser of it. His mind and hand went together: And what he thought, he uttered with that easiness, that wee have scarce received from him a blot in his papers. But it is not our province, who onely gather his works, and give them you, to praise him. It is yours that reade him. And there we hope, to your divers capacities, you will finde enough, both to draw, and hold you: for his wit can no more lie hid, then it could be lost. Reade him, therefore; and againe, and againe: And if then you doe not like him, surely you are in some manifest danger, not to understand him. And so we leave you to other of his Friends, whom if you need, can bee your guides: if you neede them not, you can leade your selves, and others. And such Readers we wish him.

English playwright and poet Ben Jonson's admiration for Shakespeare, his friend and contemporary, was warm but not uncritical. On reading the testimony by Heminge and Condell he could not withhold a certain scorn. This excerpt is taken from Timber *(in* Works, *1640).*

I *remember*, the Players have often mentioned it as an honour to *Shakespeare*, that in his writing, (whatsoever he penn'd) hee never blotted out line. My answer hath beene, would he had blotted a thousand. Which they thought a malevolent speech. I had not told posterity this, but for their ignorance, who choose that circumstance to commend their friend by, wherein he most faulted. And to justifie mine owne candor, (for I lov'd the man, and doe honour his memory (on this side Idolatry) as much as any.) Hee was (indeed) honest, and of an open, and free nature: had an excellent *Phantsie*; brave notions, and gentle expressions: wherein hee flow'd with that facility, that sometime it was necessary he should be stop'd: *Sufflminandus erat*; as *Augustus* said of *Haterius*. His wit was in his owne power; would the rule of it had beene so too. Many times hee fell into those things, could not escape laughter: As when hee said in the person of *Caesar*, one speaking to him; *Caesar thou dost me wrong.* Hee replyed: *Caesar did never wrong, but with just cause* and such like: which were ridiculous. But hee redeemed his vices, with his vertues. There was ever more in him to be praysed, then to be pardoned.

This was not the first time that Jonson had sniped at Shakespeare. When he visited Scottish poet William Drummond (1585–1649) in 1618 Jonson had this to say:

Sheakspear in a play brought in a number of men saying they had suffered Shipwrack in Bohemia, wher ther is no Sea neer by some 100 Miles.

Playgoers' Testimony

Thousands of Londoners went to see Shakespeare's plays, but very few of them recorded their impressions. In February 1602 a law student named John Manningham went to see a play— Twelfth Night—*performed in Middle Temple Hall, and wrote this in his diary (now in the British Library, London).*

At our feast wee had a play called Twelve night or what you will, much like the commedy of errors or Menechmi in plautus but most like and neere to that in Italian called Inganni a good practise in it to make the steward beleeve his Lady widdowe was in Love wth him by counterfayting a lettr as from his Lady in generall tearmes telling him what shee liked best in him and prescribing his gesture in smiling his apparraile etc. And then when he came to practise making him beleeve they tooke him to be mad.

A more assiduous theatergoer was Simon Forman, doctor, magician, and amateur psychiatrist. In April 1611 (1610 is a mistake) he went to see Macbeth *and left a detailed and thoughtful description of it (also in the British Library).*

In Mackbeth at the Glob, 1610, the 20 of Aprill [Saturday], ther was to be observed, firste, howe Mackbeth and Bancko, 2 noble men of Scotland, Ridinge thorowe a wod, the[r] stode before them 3 women feiries or Nimphes, And saluted Mackbeth, sayinge, 3 tyms unto him, haille Mackbeth, king of Codon; for thou shalt be a kinge, but shalt beget No kinges, etc. Then said Bancko, What all to Mackbeth And nothing to me. Yes, said the nimphes, haille to thee Bancko, thou shalt beget kinges, yet be no kinge. And so they departed & cam to the Courte of Scotland to Dunkin king of Scotes, and yt was in the dais of Edward the Confessor. And Dunkin bad them both kindly wellcome, And made Mackbeth forth with Prince of Northumberland, and sent him hom to his own castell, and appointed Mackbeth to provid for him, for he would sup with him the next dai at night, & did soe. And Mackebeth contrived to kill Dunkin, & thorowe the persuasion of his wife did that night Murder the kinge in his owne Castell, beinge his guest. And ther were many prodigies seen that night & the dai before. And when Mack Beth had murdred the kinge, the blod on his handes could not be washed of by Any meanes, nor from his wives handes, which handled the bloddi daggers in hiding them, By which means they became both moch amazed & Affronted. The murder being knowen, Dunkins 2 sonns fled, the on to England, the [other to] Walles, to save them selves, they being fled, they were supposed guilty of the murder of their father, which was nothinge so. Then was Mackbeth crowned kinge, and then he for feare of Banko, his old companion, that he should beget kinges but be no kinge him selfe, he contrived the death of Banko, and caused him to be Murdred on the way as he Rode. The next night, beinge at supper with his noble men whom he had bid to a feaste to the which also Banco should have com, he began to speake of Noble Banco, and to wish that he wer ther. And as he thus did, standing up to drincke a Carouse to him, the ghoste of Banco came and sate down in his cheier behind him. And he turninge About to sit down Again sawe the goste of Banco, which fronted him so, that he fell into a great passion of fear and fury, Utterynge many wordes about his murder, by which, when they hard that Banco was Murdred they Suspected Mackbet.

Then Mackdove fled to England to the kinges sonn, And soe they Raised an Army, And cam into Scotland, and at Dunston Anyse overthrue Mackbet. In the meantyme whille Macdovee was in England, Mackbet slewe Mackdoves wife & children, and after in the battelle Mackdove slewe Mackbet.

Observe Also howe Mackbetes quen did Rise in the night in her slepe, & walke and talked and confessed all, & the docter noted her wordes.

Macbeth, as played by a Mr. Anderson.

Mᴿ ANDERSON as MACBETH.

Shakespeare Criticism

Shakespeare criticism began in England with the work of the neoclassical writers Alexander Pope (1688–1744) and Samuel Johnson (1709–84), who won credence for the idea that the playwright's genius allowed him to rise above the rules drawn up by Aristotle in his Poetics, *particularly those relating to the structure and purpose of tragedy.*

To the Reader.

This Figure, that thou here seest put,
  It was for gentle Shakespeare cut:
Wherein the Grauer had a strife
  with Nature, to out-doo the life:
O, could he but haue drawne his wit
  As well in brasse, as he hath hit
His face; the Print would then surpasse
  All, that was euer writ in brasse.
But, since he cannot, Reader, looke
  Not on his Picture, but his Booke.

In the 19th century German writers Johann Wolfgang von Goethe, Friedrich von Schlegel, and Johann Ludwig Tieck waxed enthusiastic over Shakespeare's work. In England William Wordsworth expressed the belief that the sonnets held the key to Shakespeare's heart. John Keats identified in a letter what he termed his "negative capability…that is, when a man is capable of being in uncertainties, mysteries, doubts, without any irritable reaching after fact and reason." And Samuel Taylor Coleridge wrote numerous essays on the plays, emphasizing the often remarkable qualities of his female characters. For him, Shakespeare was as mysterious and elusive as Proteus, god of the sea and metamorphosis. In France Stendhal expressed great admiration for Shakespeare, whom he saw as the master of prose drama, while Victor Hugo, whose plays show the undeniable influence of the great Elizabethan, was even more strongly impressed by him. Hugo acclaimed the universality of Shakespeare's genius in his work *William Shakespeare,* written in 1864.

In the 20th century criticism was dominated by A. C. Bradley, who in 1904 published a series of lectures devoted to the psychological study of the main characters in the great tragedies *Hamlet, Othello, King Lear,* and *Macbeth* under the title *Shakespearean Tragedy.* After the war a Cambridge University professor, L. C. Knights, wrote ironically about the tendency of critics to treat fictitious characters as if they were entirely real

Note from the First Folio, 1623 (left).

King *Lear Weeping over the Body of Cordelia*, an 18th-century engraving after James Barry.

human beings in a famous article published in 1933, entitled "How Many Children Had Lady Macbeth?" He articulated the idea that Shakespeare was, first and foremost, a dramatic poet and that his work had to be analyzed through its images and words. This aspect of his writing then drew greater critical attention, specifically in Caroline Spurgeon's book *Shakespeare's Imagery, and What It Tells Us* (1935) and the many essays published by George Wilson Knight (1933).

The trend in the 1930s and 1940s was to return to the study of historical background, for example in the work of Eustace M. Tillyard, *The Elizabethan World Picture* (1943). In his eyes, Shakespeare was complying with Tudor ideology when he wrote his historical dramas, presenting the duke of Richmond (Henry VII), for example,

in his official light as providential savior of an English nation torn apart by the horrors of civil war. These theories are heavily disputed today, particularly by those who think in terms of cultural materialism, and see Shakespeare, contrarily, as a writer who sympathized with the oppressed (women and the poor) and whose superficial allegiances masked criticism of the mechanisms of power.

In France Shakespeare criticism found its expression in the work of Henri Fluchère, *Shakespeare Dramaturge Elisabéthain* ("Shakespeare, Elizabethan dramatist"), published in 1947. A disciple of the Cambridge school led by Knights and Frank R. Leavis, and influenced by T. S. Eliot's essays, Fluchère concentrated on an analysis of the poetic quality of Shakespeare's work rather than of the author's life and the psychology of his characters. "It is only the man's work and not his actions and behavior that concern us.... The man and the mystery about him have relegated his work to second place for too long." Meanwhile, in England, Allardyce Nicoll and Glynne Wickham studied the organization of the theaters and companies; Kenneth Muir and Geoffrey Bullough researched the sources of the plays, which helped extend the traditional approach to Shakespeare's work and gave access to new information—both historical and iconographic—that threw light on Shakespeare's contribution to the theater of his time.

The Cold War period and the rise of existentialism and Marxism gave birth to materialist analyses of Shakespeare's drama, such as *Shakespeare Our Contemporary* (1964) by the Polish writer Jan Kott. Kott's ideas greatly influenced the productions of the 1960s, in particular those of Peter Brook, who drew on them considerably. In Kott's eyes there were no good or bad kings, only the implacable steamroller of history crushing individuals like an inhuman machine. This materialist critical approach, influenced predominantly by Karl Marx and Bertolt Brecht, developed significantly with the work of Robert Weimann, *Shakespeare and Popular Tradition in the Theatre*, published in German in 1967 and in English translation in 1978, inviting comparison with *Rabelais and Popular Culture in the Middle Ages and the Renaissance* (1970) by the Russian Mikhail Bakhtin.

Psychoanalysts have also taken a great interest in Shakespeare's writing, starting with Sigmund Freud himself, who numbered the playwright's works

Lady Macbeth steeling herself for the murder of Duncan, a late 18th-century engraving after Richard Westall.

among his bedside books, often referred to him, and even wrote important articles on his plays. Freud's disciple Ernest Jones explained Hamlet's puzzling hesitation in enacting the vengeance demanded by his dead father in terms of the Oedipus complex: Hamlet hated Claudius and at the same time envied him for occupying the place by Queen Gertrude's side that he himself secretly desired. In the aftermath of this now classic study, essays and articles from the psychoanalytic standpoint have multiplied. Among the more recent are Jacques Lacan's articles on *Hamlet*, Bernard Sichère's *Le Nom de Shakespeare* ("The name of Shakespeare"), and *Avec Shakespeare* ("With Shakespeare") by the psychoanalyst Daniel Sibony.

In the last fifteen years Shakespeare criticism has been enlivened, not to say disturbed, by a variety of schools of thought: feminism, deconstructionism (notably the theories of the French philosopher Jacques Derrida), and New Historicism. This last movement, spearheaded by Stephen Greenblatt, author of *Renaissance Self-Fashioning* (1980), aims to situate Shakespeare's work in its historical context, in relation to his contemporaries, and as part of the European Renaissance. All three currents of thought have between them produced a proliferation of articles, books, and new editions of Shakespeare.

Less eyecatching, but no less important, are the advances in textual criticism made by scholars examining the varied technical processes behind the texts of the different editions of Shakespeare, culminating in the publication of the New Oxford Shakespeare, edited by Stanley Wells and Gary Taylor (*A Textual Companion*, 1987, and *The Complete Works*, 1986).

Though opinion on the investigations of these two specialists is divided, the immensity of the task accomplished makes the edition an essential tool of reference.

In *Shakespeare, Les Feux de l'Envie* ("Shakespeare, the fires of desire") published in 1990, René Girard discusses a number of Shakespeare's plays in terms of the theory elaborated in his earlier works, the principle of mimetic desire and the rites of violence in primitive societies. Girard's book has not been unanimously well received by university critics— evidence of the extent to which, as James Joyce suggested in *Ulysses,* Shakespeare is being used as an ideological pawn.

More recent British and American criticism has tended to become increasingly specialized and written in a increasingly technical language not easily accessible to the layperson. The most radical theorists have abandoned the quest for "truth" altogether, and believe that "meaning" fluctuates with time and culture and that Shakespeare's plays today are necessarily part of today's ideological strategies. Terence Hawkes, for instance, in *Meaning by Shakespeare,* claims that we "use" *Hamlet,* rather as Hamlet "used" "The Murder of Gonzago" to prove something to ourselves in our world. "Perhaps," he says, "its probing of the relation between art and social life, role-playing on stage and role-playing in society, appears so powerfully to offer an adequate account of important aspects of our own experience that it ends by constructing them. In other words, *Hamlet* crucially helps to determine how we perceive and respond to the world in which we live."

François Laroque

Shakespeare Multiplied: The Changing Perspective of Criticism

Every generation recreates Shakespeare in its own image. What one age sees as his supreme merit, another ignores in the search for something quite different. It is a measure of the extraordinary complexity of Shakespeare's genius that, uniquely among great artists, he can survive this treatment.

The Classical Shakespeare

During the later 17th and most of the 18th centuries, criticism of Shakespeare tended to focus on his universality— his understanding of every type of human being and ability to express every kind of emotion. For these writers, Shakespeare was an untaught child of nature who seemed to have produced masterpieces almost without knowing it. John Dryden (1631–1700) was the first English literary critic. Written only fifty years after Shakespeare's death, Dryden's comments seem impressively balanced and objective.

To begin then with Shakespeare; he was the man who of all Modern, and perhaps Ancient Poets, had the largest and most comprehensive soul. All the Images of Nature were still present to him, and he drew them not laboriously, but luckily: when he describes any thing, you more than see it, you feel it too. Those who accuse him to have wanted learning, give him the greater commendation: he was naturally learn'd; he needed not the spectacles of Books to read Nature; he look'd inwards, and found her there. I cannot say he is every where alike; were he so, I should do him injury to compare him with the greatest of Mankind. He is many times flat, insipid; his Comick wit degenerating into clenches [puns], his serious swelling into Bombast. But he is always great, when some great occasion is presented to him: no man can say he ever had a fit subject for his wit, and did not then raise himself as high above the rest of Poets.

Of Dramatic Poesie, 1668

Nicholas Rowe (1674–1718) was Shakespeare's first editor and biographer.

His Plays are properly to be distinguish'd only into Comedies and Tragedies. Those which are called Histories, and even some of his Comedies, are really Tragedies, with a run or mixture of Comedy amongst 'em. That way of Trage-Comedy was the common Mistake of that Age, and is indeed become so agreeable to the English Tast, that tho' the severer Critiques among us cannot bear it, yet the generality of our Audiences seem to be better pleas'd with it than with an exact Tragedy. *The Merry Wives of Windsor, The Comedy of Errors,* and *The Taming of the Shrew* are all pure Comedy; the rest, however they are call'd, have something of both Kinds.

'Tis not very easie to determine which way of Writing he was most Excellent in. There is certainly a great deal of Entertainment in his Comical Humours; and tho' they did not then strike at all Ranks of People, as the Satyr of the present Age has taken the Liberty to do, yet there is a pleasing and a well-distinguish'd Variety in those Characters which he thought fit to meddle with. Falstaff is allow'd by every body to be a Master-piece; the Character is always well-sustain'd, tho' drawn out into the length of three Plays; and even the Account of his Death, given by his Old Landlady Mrs. Quickly, in the first

Portia's garden from *The Merchant of Venice,* an engraving of 1795 after William Hodges. Its classical design is inspired by the paintings of Nicolas Poussin (1594–1665).

Act of *Henry V*, tho' it be extremely Natural, is yet as diverting as any Part of his Life.

Some Account of the Life of Mr. William Shakespeare, 1709

English poet and critic Alexander Pope (1688–1744) edited an edition of Shakespeare's works that was published in 1725. This excerpt is from his preface.

His Characters are so much Nature her self, that 'tis a sort of injury to call them by so distant a name as Copies of her. Those of other Poets have a constant resemblance, which shews that they receiv'd them from one another, and were but multiplyers of the same image: each picture like a mock-rainbow is but the reflection of a reflection. But every single character in Shakespear is as

David Garrick as Richard III, an engraving after William Hogarth, c. 1745, showing the king awakening from his nightmare before the battle.

much an Individual, as those in Life itself; it is as impossible to find any two alike; and such as from their relation or affinity in any respect appear most to be Twins, will upon comparison be found remarkably distinct. To this life and variety of Character, we must add the wonderful Preservation of it; which is such throughout his plays, that had all the Speeches been printed without the very names of the Persons, I believe one might have apply'd them with certainty to every speaker.

Works of Shakespear, 1725

Samuel Johnson (1709–84) also published a version of Shakespeare in which he summed up the neoclassical view. Largely unresponsive to his poetry (unlike Pope), he valued Shakespeare for his ability to generalize human nature and to dramatize moral choices.

Nothing can please many, and please long, but just representations of general nature. Particular manners can be known to few, and therefore few only can judge how nearly they are copied. The irregular combinations of fanciful invention may delight a-while, by that novelty of which the common satiety of life sends us all in quest; but the pleasures of sudden wonder are soon exhausted, and the mind can only repose on the stability of truth.

Shakespeare is above all writers, at least above all modern writers, the poet of nature; the poet that holds up to his readers a faithful mirror of manners and of life. His characters are not modified by the customs of particular places, unpractised by the rest of the world; by the peculiarities of studies or professions, which can operate but upon small numbers; or by the accidents of transient fashions or temporary opinions: they are the genuine progeny of common humanity, such as the world will always supply, and observation will always find. His persons act and speak by the influence of those general passions and principles by which all minds are agitated, and the whole system of life is continued in motion. In the writings of other poets a character is too often an individual; in those of Shakespeare it is commonly a species.

Shakespeare's Plays, 1765

The Romantic Shakespeare

The 19th century saw a drastic reversal in the neoclassical position. Shakespeare's indifference to the classical rules, his spontaneous expression of extreme emotion, and above all, his language, became for this new generation the essence of his genius. For these thinkers Shakespeare is a poet to be read, not a playwright to be experienced in the theater. English essayist and critic Charles Lamb (1775–1834) is credited with helping to revive Shakespeare's popularity.

It may seem a paradox, but I cannot help being of opinion that the plays of Shakspeare are less calculated for performance on a stage, than those of almost any other dramatist whatever. Their distinguishing excellence is a reason that they should be so. There is so much in them, which comes not under the province of acting, with which eye, and tone, and gesture, have nothing to do.... The sublime images, the poetry alone, is that which is present to our minds in the reading.

So to see Lear acted,—to see an old man tottering about the stage with a walking-stick, turned out of doors by his daughters in a rainy night, has nothing in it but what is painful and disgusting. We want to take him into shelter and relieve him. That is all the feeling which the acting of Lear ever produced in me. But the Lear of Shakspeare cannot be acted. The contemptible machinery by which they mimic the storm which he goes out in, is not more inadequate to represent the horrors of the real elements, than any actor can be to represent Lear: they might more easily propose to personate the Satan of Milton upon a stage, or one of Michael Angelo's terrible figures. The greatness of Lear is not in corporal dimension, but in intellectual: the explosions of his passion are terrible as a volcano: they are storms turning up and disclosing to the bottom that sea, his mind, with all its vast riches. It is his mind which is laid bare.

On the Tragedies of Shakespeare, 1811

Lamb's friend the poet and philosopher Samuel Taylor Coleridge (1772–1845)

believed Shakespeare to be a sublime and exalted thinker whose very obscurity is a mark of his genius.

It has been before observed that images, however beautiful, though faithfully copied from nature, and as accurately represented in words, do not of themselves characterize the poet. They become proofs of original genius only as far as they are modified by a predominant passion; or by associated thoughts or images awakened by that passion; or when they have the effect of reducing multitude to unity, or succession to an instant; or lastly, when a human and intellectual life is transferred to them from the poet's own spirit.

Biographia Literaria, 1817

Shakspeare possessed the chief, if not every, requisite of a poet,—deep feeling and exquisite sense of beauty, both as exhibited to the eye in the combinations of form, and to the ear in sweet and appropriate melody; that these feelings were under the command

This inkwell featuring a bust of Shakespeare belonged to John Keats.

of his own will; that in his very first productions he projected his mind out of his own particular being, and felt, and made others feel, on subjects no way connected with himself, except by force of contemplation and that sublime faculty by which a great mind becomes that, on which it meditates.

Lectures, 1818

Shakspeare is of no age. It is idle to endeavour to support his phrases by quotations from Ben Jonson, Beaumont and Fletcher, &c. His language is entirely his own, and the younger dramatists imitated him. The construction of Shakspeare's sentences, whether in verse or prose, is the necessary and homogeneous vehicle of his peculiar manner of thinking. His is not the style of the age....

I believe Shakspeare was not a whit more intelligible in his own day than he is now to an educated man, except for a few local allusions of no consequence. As I said, he is of no age—nor, I may add, of any religion, or party, or profession. The body and substance of his works came out of the unfathom-able depths of his own oceanic mind: his observation and reading, which was considerable, supplied him with the drapery of his figures.

Table Talk, 1836

The comments of poet John Keats (1795–1826) about Shakespeare consist of remarks in letters or in the margins of his copy of the plays, and he made no attempt to develop them. Yet they are among the most perceptive made by any critic, and are especially valuable coming from a poet of such genius. He was particularly struck by Shakespeare's apparent ability to lose his own identity in *that of other beings, an ability which for him lay at the root of poetry.*

Several things dovetailed in my mind, & at once it struck me, what quality went to form a Man of Achievement, especially in Literature, & which Shakespeare possessed so enormously— I mean *Negative Capability,* that is when a man is capable of being in uncertainties, Mysteries, doubts, without any irritable reaching after fact & reason.

Letter of 21 December 1817

The excellence of every art is its intensity, capable of making all disagreeables evaporate from their being in close relationship with Beauty and Truth. Examine "King Lear," and you will find this exemplified throughout.

Letter of 28 December 1817

WRITTEN BEFORE REREADING KING LEAR
O golden-tongued Romance with
    serene lute!
Fair plumed Syren! Queen of far away!
Leave melodizing on this wintry day,
Shut up thine olden volume, and be
    mute.
Adieu! for once again the fierce dispute,
Betwixt damnation and impassioned
    clay
Must I burn through; once more assay
The bitter-sweet of this Shakespearean
    fruit.
Chief Poet! and ye clouds of Albion,
Begetters of our deep eternal theme,
When through the old oak forest I am
    gone
Let me not wander in a barren dream,
But when I am consumed with the Fire,
Give me new Phoenix-wings to fly at
    my desire.

22 January 1818

It was English essayist William Hazlitt (1778–1830) who began seriously to explore the psychological aspect of Shakespeare's plays, an approach that dominated criticism throughout the 19th century and up to our own time. The technique of character analysis was born.

Each of his characters is as much itself, and as absolutely independent of the rest, as well as of the author, as if they were living persons, not fictions of the mind. The poet may be said, for the time, to identify himself with the character he wishes to represent, and to pass from one to another, like the same soul successively animating different bodies. By an art like that of the ventriloquist, he throws his imagination out of himself, and makes every word appear to proceed from the mouth of the person in whose name it is given. His plays alone are properly expressions of the passions, not descriptions of them. His characters are real beings of flesh and blood; they speak like men, not like authors. One might suppose that he had stood by at the time and overheard what passed. As in our dreams we hold conversations with ourselves, make remarks, or communicate intelligence, and have no idea of the answer which we shall receive, and which we ourselves make, till we hear it: so the dialogues

H amlet and his father's ghost, seen through Romantic eyes. A late 18th-century engraving after a painting by Henry Fuseli.

in Shakespeare are carried on without any consciousness of what is to follow, without any appearance of preparation or premeditation. The gusts of passion come and go like sounds of music borne on the wind. Nothing is made out by formal inference and analogy, by climax and antithesis: all comes, or seems to come, immediately from nature. Each object and circumstance exists in his mind, as it would have existed in reality: each several train of thought and feeling goes on of itself, without confusion or effort. In the world of his imagination, everything has a life, a place and being of its own!

Lectures on the English Poets, 1818

English literary critic Andrew Cecil Bradley (1851–1935) was the supreme practitioner of character analysis, and his detailed comments on individual Shakespearean characters are still valuable. But when he attempted to define the nature of Shakespearean tragedy he propounded a theory of the hero's "tragic flaw," which, while archetypically Romantic, may now seem as remote from our time as it does from Shakespeare's.

His tragic characters are made of the stuff we find within ourselves and within the persons who surround them. But, by an intensification of the life which they share with others, they are raised above them; and the greatest are raised so far that, if we fully realise all that is implied in their words and actions, we become conscious that in real life we have known scarcely any one resembling them. Some, like Hamlet and Cleopatra, have genius. Others, like Othello, Lear, Macbeth,

Coriolanus, are built on the grand scale; and desire, passion, or will attains in them a terrible force. In almost all we observe a marked one-sidedness, a predisposition in some particular direction; a total incapacity, in certain circumstances, of resisting the force which draws in this direction; a fatal tendency to identify the whole being with one interest, object, passion, or habit of mind. This, it would seem, is, for Shakespeare, the fundamental tragic trait.... It is a fatal gift, but it carries with it a touch of greatness; and when there is joined to it nobility of mind, or genius, or immense force, we realise the full power and reach of the soul, and the conflict in which it engages acquires that magnitude which stirs not only sympathy and pity, but admiration, terror, and awe....

In the circumstances where we see the hero placed, his tragic trait, which is also his greatness, is fatal to him. To meet these circumstances something is required which a smaller man might have given, but which the hero cannot give. He errs, by action or omission; and his error, joining with other causes, brings on him ruin.

Hence, in the first place, a Shakespearean tragedy is never, like some miscalled tragedies, depressing. No one ever closes the book with the feeling that man is a poor mean creature. He may be wretched and he may be awful, but he is not small. His lot may be heart-rending and mysterious, but it is not contemptible. The most confirmed of cynics ceases to be a cynic while he reads these plays. And with this greatness of the tragic hero (which is not always confined to him) is connected, secondly, what I venture to describe as the centre of the tragic impression. This central feeling is the impression of waste. With Shakespeare, at any rate, the pity and fear which are stirred by the tragic story seem to unite with, and even to merge in, a profound sense of sadness and mystery, which is due to this impression of waste. "What a piece of work is man," we cry; "so much more beautiful and so much more terrible than we knew! Why should he be so if this beauty and greatness only tortures itself and throws itself away?" We seem to have before us a type of the mystery of the whole world, the tragic fact which extends far beyond the limits of tragedy.

Shakespearean Tragedy, 1904

Dissenting Views

There have always been those who thought Shakespeare overrated. Ironically, these critics include two of the greatest minds in European literature—French writer Voltaire (1694–1778) and Russian novelist Lev Nikolayevich Tolstoy (1828–1910). According to Voltaire, Shakespeare was a barbarian. He did not deny his talent, but was revolted by his lack of classical decorum.

Shakespeare boasted a strong, fruitful genius. He was natural and sublime, but had not so much as a single spark of good taste, or knew one rule of the drama.

Philosophical Letters, 1733

Everywhere, the common people are pleased by astonishing events; they love to see scene changes, coronations of kings, processions, fights, murders, witches, ceremonies, weddings, burials; they rush to these things in crowds and carry along with them others who are ready to forgive their enormous faults if there are also a few beauties, and even if there are not.

Letter to the Académie Française, 1776

[On *Hamlet*] This vulgar and barbarous play would not be supported by the lowest public of France or Italy. In it Hamlet goes mad in the second act, and his mistress in the third; the prince kills his mistress's father, pretending to kill a rat, and the heroine throws herself into the river. Her grave is dug on the stage; the grave-diggers utter doubtful pleasantries worthy of them, while holding skulls in their hands; prince Hamlet replies to their abominable vulgarities with no less disgusting idiocies. Meanwhile, one of the characters conquers Poland. Hamlet, his mother, and his stepfather drink together on the stage; they sing at the table, quarrel, fight, and kill each other. One would take this work to be the fruit of the inspiration of a drunken savage.

An Appeal to All the Nations of Europe, 1761

Tolstoy's objection to Shakespeare was partly that his language was unnatural, but mainly that he had no significant moral message.

I remember the astonishment I felt when I first read Shakespeare. I expected to receive a powerful aesthetic pleasure, but having read, one after the other, works regarded as his best, *King Lear, Romeo and Juliet, Hamlet,* and *Macbeth,* not only did I feel no delight, but I felt an irresistible repulsion and tedium, and doubted as to whether I was senseless in feeling works regarded as the summit of perfection by the whole of the civilized world to be trivial and positively bad, or whether the significance that this civilized world attributes to the works of Shakespeare was itself senseless. My consternation was increased by the fact that I always keenly felt the beauties of poetry in every form; then why should artistic works recognized by the whole world as those of a genius—the works of Shakespeare—not only fail to please me, but be disagreeable to me?...

All his characters speak, not their own, but always one and the same Shakespearean pretentious and unnatural language, in which not only they could not speak, but in which no living man ever has spoken or does speak.... From his first words, exaggeration is seen: the exaggeration of events, the exaggeration of emotion, and the exaggeration of effects. One sees at once that he does not believe in what he says, that it is of no necessity to him, that he invents the events he describes and is indifferent to his characters—that he has conceived them only for the stage and therefore makes them do and say only what may strike his public, and so we do not believe either in the events or in the actions or in the sufferings of the characters.

He alone can write a drama who has got something to say to men, and that something of the greatest importance for them: about man's relation to God, to the Universe, to the All, the Eternal, the Infinite. But when, thanks to the German theories about objective art, the idea was established that for the drama this was quite unnecessary, then it became obvious how a writer like Shakespeare—who had not developed in his mind the religious convictions proper to his time, who, in fact, had no convictions at all, but heaped up in his drama all possible events, horrors, fooleries, discussions, and effects—could appear to be a dramatic writer of the greatest genius.

But these are all external reasons. The fundamental inner cause of Shakespeare's fame was and is this—that his dramas ...corresponded to the irreligious and immoral frame of mind of the upper classes of his time and ours.

Shakespeare and the Drama, 1906

Like Tolstoy, English playwright and drama critic for the Saturday Review *George Bernard Shaw (1856–1950) was irritated by the uncritical adulation given to Shakespeare, whom he considered (in comparison with such writers as Henrik Ibsen and himself) to be lacking in ideas and depressingly bourgeois in his attitude to social questions.*

A *Study for King Lear,* painted c. 1773 by Sir Joshua Reynolds.

Once or twice we scent an anticipation of the crudest side of Ibsen's polemics on the Woman Question, as in *All's Well that Ends Well,* where the man cuts as meanly selfish a figure beside his enlightened lady doctor wife as Helmer beside Nora; or in *Cymbeline,* where Posthumus, having, as he believes, killed his wife for inconstancy, speculates for a moment on what his life would have been worth if the same standard of continence had been applied to himself. And certainly no modern study of the voluptuous temperament, and the spurious heroism and heroinism which its ecstasies produce, can add much to *Antony and Cleopatra,* unless it were some sense of the spuriousness on the author's part. But search for statesmanship, or even citizenship, or any sense of the commonwealth, material or spiritual, and you will not find the making of a decent vestryman or curate in the whole horde. As to faith, hope, courage, conviction, or any of the true heroic qualities, you find nothing but death made sensational, despair made stage-sublime, sex made romantic, and barrenness covered up by sentimentality and the mechanical lilt of blank verse.

All that you miss in Shakespear you find in Bunyan, to whom the true heroic came quite obviously and naturally. The world was to him a more terrible place than it was to Shakespear; but he saw through it a path at the end of which a man might look not only forward to the Celestial City, but back on his life and say:—"Tho' with great difficulty I am got hither, yet now I do not repent me of all the trouble I have been at to arrive where I am. My sword I give

to him that shall succeed me in my pilgrimage, and my courage and skill to him that can get them." The heart vibrates like a bell to such an utterance as this: to turn from it to "Out, out, brief candle," and "The rest is silence," and "We are such stuff as dreams are made of; and our little life is rounded by a sleep" is to turn from life, strength, resolution, morning air and eternal youth, to the terrors of a drunken nightmare.

Saturday Review
January 1896

And then Touchstone, with his rare jests about the knight that swore by his honor they were good pancakes! Who would endure such humor from anyone but Shakespear?—an Eskimo would demand his money back if a modern author offered him such fare. And the comfortable old Duke, symbolical of the British villa dweller, who likes to find "sermons in stones and good in everything," and then to have a good dinner! This unvenerable impostor, expanding on his mixed diet of pious twaddle and venison, rouses my worst passions. Even when Shakespear, in his efforts to be a social philosopher, does rise for an instant to the level of a sixth-rate Kingsley, his solemn self-complacency infuriates me. And yet, so wonderful is his art, that it is not easy to disentangle what is unbearable from what is irresistible. Orlando one moment says:

> Whate'er you are
> That in this desert inaccessible
> Under the shade of melancholy
>   boughs
> Lose and neglect the creeping hours
>   of time,

which, though it indicates a thoroughly unhealthy imagination, and would have been impossible to, for instance, Chaucer, is yet magically fine of its kind. The next moment he tacks on lines which would have revolted Mr. Pecksniff:

If ever you have looked on better days,
If ever been where bells have knolled to church,
    [*How perfectly the atmosphere of the rented pew is caught in this incredible line!*]
If ever sat at any good man's feast,
If ever from your eyelids wiped—

I really shall get sick if I quote any more of it. Was ever such canting, snivelling, hypocritical unctuousness exuded by an actor anxious to shew that he was above his profession, and was a thoroughly respectable man in private life?

Saturday Review
December 1896

In modern times Shakespeare has come under fire from those who, for all their admiration, prefer to stay (in Ben Jonson's words) "this side idolatry," and feel bound to point out that he had his limitations. For Shakespearean scholar and editor Gary Taylor, as for Tolstoy and Shaw, these limitations are largely moral ones.

To take just one example, *Measure for Measure* tells the story of a puritanical governor who sets out to eliminate sexual corruption in Vienna. Shakespeare tells the story in a way that repeatedly undercuts this ambition. Angelo, the governor, himself succumbs to lust; the most visible victims of his crusade are a likable young engaged couple, guilty of nothing more heinous than consummation before consecration (dessert before saying grace). By concentrating upon the hypocritical governor and the unlucky lovers, Shakespeare distracts attention from the real focus of sexual corruption, Viennese prostitution. The sex industry

John Everett Millais's famous painting of the death of Ophelia (1851–2) is a literal rendering of the queen's description in *Hamlet*.

is represented in his play by a…crew of harmless comics: dumb customer, daffy pimp, dizzy madam. The names themselves assure us that we have entered the world of happy whoredom. But where, pray tell, are the prostitutes?

Shakespeare shows us the customers and the management, but the sexual work force itself, the women who ride up and down the shaft to the coal mines of prostitution, them we never see, never hear, hardly hear of. The worst punishment that can be devised for Lucio, at the play's end, a punishment many modern critics consider neurotically severe (on the Duke's part or Shakespeare's), is "Marrying a punk"—being forced to husband a prostitute he had impregnated. Likewise, in *Pericles* we see the husband-and-wife duo of brothel owners comically complaining about the local whore shortage, and we see their eager underling Bolt (a name both phallic and functional, since he bolts the door); but nary a prostitute do we see. The management buys and then tries to sell Marina; but she, in a delectable little dramatic fantasy, moralizes the lust out of her customers, so that they pay her for sermons instead of sex. Indeed, one of them, who happens happily to be the most eligible bachelor in town, falls in love with her and, in due course, proposes marriage.

Shakespeare wasted no sympathy on the women lured or conned or forced into prostitution. The working women who do appear in his plays are accused of murdering their customers outright (Doll Tearsheet, in *Henry IV, Part 2*) or of murdering them piecemeal, with disease (Phrynia and Timandra, in *Timon of Athens*), in both cases

without compunction or compulsion. Shakespeare's contemporary Thomas Middleton could sympathize with the "Distressed needlewomen and trade-fallne wives," the "poore spirits" and "poore shifting sisters," "hungry things" caught on the "hooke" baited by urban pimps; but Shakespeare himself never considers, or asks his audience to consider, the circumstances or motives of such women.

Shakespeare sees prostitution from the outside, or rather from the male side, the side of the customer or the pimp; the women either do not exist at all (as in *Measure for Measure* and *Pericles*) or deserve contempt (as in *Henry IV, Part 2* and *Timon of Athens*). Curiously, unrealistically, they are never young, never beautiful, never genuinely alluring. To make them attractive would be to admit their power.

Reinventing Shakespeare
1990

The Modern Shakespeare

As the Shakespeare industry has gathered momentum in the 20th century, the number of perspectives on his work has multiplied. He has been interpreted by Freudians, Marxists, anthropologists, linguists, feminists, philosophers, and literary theorists of every persuasion.

Polish writer Jan Kott fought against the Nazis in the Polish underground movement and then suffered under Stalinism. His Shakespeare is a realist, not a Romantic.

Every historical period finds in him what it is looking for and what it wants to see. A reader or spectator in the mid-20th century interprets *Richard III* through his own experiences. He cannot do otherwise. And that is why he is not terrified—or rather, not amazed—at Shakespeare's cruelty. He views the struggle for power and the mutual slaughter of the characters far more calmly than did many generations of spectators and critics in the 19th century. More calmly, or, at any rate, more rationally. Cruel death, suffered by most dramatis personae, is not regarded today as an aesthetic necessity, or as an essential rule in tragedy in order to produce catharsis, or even as a specific characteristic of Shakespeare's genius. The violent deaths of the principal characters are now regarded rather as an historical necessity, or as something altogether natural.

Even in *Titus Andronicus*, written, or rewritten, by Shakespeare probably in the same year as *King Richard III*, modern audiences see much more than the ludicrous and grotesque accumulation of needless horrors which 19th century critics found in it. And when *Titus Andronicus* received a production like that by Peter Brook, today's audiences were ready to applaud the general slaughter in act five no less enthusiastically than Elizabethan coppersmiths, tailors, butchers, and soldiers had done. In those days the play was one of the greatest theatrical successes.

By discovering in Shakespeare's plays problems that are relevant to our own time, modern audiences often, unexpectedly, find themselves near to the Elizabethans; or at least are in the position to understand them well. This is particularly true of the histories.

Shakespeare Our Contemporary
1964

Theatrical Convention

According to German critic Levin L. Schücking, it is no longer customary to stress the "naturalness" of Shakespeare's plays and to treat the characters as if they were real people. Plays are artificial constructs, with determining conventions of their own.

We must remember that our illusion in the theatre is entirely different from that of the Elizabethans.... Our drama is enacted under the tacit agreement that there are no spectators present. Only one wall, that in front of the audience, is wanting to the scene. In contrast to this, Shakespeare's stage is surrounded by the spectators on three sides. The actor may be said to stand in the midst of the audience; he is always mindful of this while he is acting, and evidently in many cases directly addresses his spectators.... This relation is evidenced by the monologue, in which the speaker, so to say, fraternizes with the audience, and the whole dramatic composition and the illusion connected with it may in this manner be absolutely destroyed. It is no longer a monologue in the proper sense—i.e., the expression of an individual who, thinking aloud, renders account of his most intimate thoughts and feelings—but a means which the author uses in order to instruct his audience about the events, or about the plans and character of the personage speaking. Such instruction and explanation is further emphasized by the form in which the actor delivering the monologue addresses the audience; e.g., "And mark how well the sequel hangs together," or "To say the truth," or "Mark me now".... This use of elements which according to our present view contradict the essence of the monologue forms a peculiar feature of Shakespeare's monologues in every period of his art, and most clearly appears in the latest products of his riper years.

Levin L. Schücking,
*Character Problems in
Shakespeare's Plays*, 1922

A Feminist Shakespeare

The rise of feminist criticism has been one of the most fruitful developments of the last few decades. Some classical authors have been found wanting. Shakespeare, however, seems to pass this test too. Here, contemporary feminist authors share their views.

Patriarchal order takes different forms… throughout the Shakespearean canon. In some comedies it weighs lightly: the power of the father or ruler can be evaded in a green world retreat or countered by the activities of the heroines. Yet at the conclusions of the comedies, the assertiveness of Kate, Rosalind, and others is muted as they declare or imply their submission to their husbands. Elsewhere patriarchy is more oppressive. Its lethal flaws are made manifest in the presentation of rape and attempted rape, in the aggressive, death-dealing feud of *Romeo and Juliet,* in the spurious manliness and empty honor that generate the tragedy of *Othello,* in the militaristic and mercantile values of the Greeks in *Troilus and Cressida* and of the Romans in *Antony and Cleopatra.* Many other plays as well reveal the high cost of patriarchal values; the men who uphold them atrophy, and the women, whether resistant or acquiescent, die. Although women may strive to resist or to correct the perversions of patriarchy, they do not succeed in altering that order, nor do they withdraw their allegiance from it. Cordelia…stands up to her father's coercion out of love for him and leads an army on behalf of his "right"; she dies a victim of a chain of brutal assertions of manhood…. In *King Lear* and elsewhere the extent to which Shakespeare aligns himself with patriarchy, merely portrays it or deliberately criticizes it remains a complex and open question, one that feminist criticism is aptly suited to address.

Carolyn Ruth Swift Lenz, Gayle
Greene, and Carol Thomas Neely,
The Woman's Part, 1980

The female who is chaste and constant is symbolically a guarantee of moral virtue in men who remain linked with her. Whether he is father, husband, lover, or brother, a man who honors his bond to a chaste constant heroine symbolically honors "feminine" ends, and thus is devoted to the right use of power. In *Love's Labour's Lost,* constancy is opposed to fickleness which arises from ignorance of one's own emotions and to egotism…. In *A Midsummer Night's Dream,* constancy is a cosmic virtue, a larger purpose containing all human purposes, and triumphant over folly and delusion. Chaste constancy swiftly becomes the cornerstone, the pivot, the crucial element in Shakespeare's morality. It has this semi-divine nature only in women because it symbolizes "feminine" qualities of harmony, community, tolerance, moral flexibility (within limits), pity, compassion, forgiveness, and loving nutritiveness. These qualities are seen as the ultimate moral goods, the things all

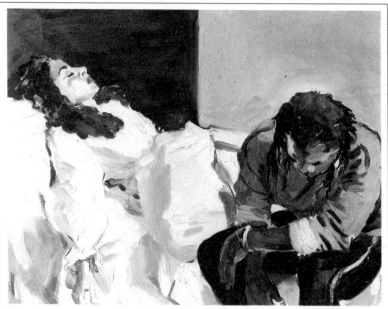

American artist Sandra Fisher's 1991 painting of actor Bob Wisdom playing Othello.

humans really need and want, or would if they were not blind. In Shakespeare's division of experience, however, men cannot be forced to revere these things. The process of coming to recognize these goods is a process of education in seeing.

Chaste constancy has several functions in the comedies from *Two Gentlemen* to *Twelfth Night* and *Much Ado*. It offers a reliable and immovable moral good that is visible in the world; thus it contrasts with male legitimacy, a set of men and institutions which claim to stand for moral good but which are untrustworthy and delusive. Second, it confers on females an equality of a sort with males. Males possess freedom and power-in-the-world; chaste constant women are bound to inlaw feminine ends and modes, but they possess moral superiority over men. This superiority is never offensive to male supremacists, however, because chaste constant heroines are utterly devoted to the male world, and usually to one man. That man is the center of her being, the only and wholly significant object of her desire. Because the man is so important to her, her entire existence is bent toward him. Her moral superiority is therefore not so much a power over him as it is an excellence, like her beauty or wit or wisdom, placed at his service.

Marilyn French
Shakespeare's Division of Experience
1982

Productions and Interpretations of Shakespeare's Plays

Following the historical reconstructions of the Victorian era, the early 20th century brought a return to the simplicity of Elizabethan stage sets. Modern productions have played a large part in the continuing success of Shakespeare's plays.

Great Productions

The Elizabethan stage of Shakespeare's day was fairly rudimentary, and the stage sets of a symbolic or merely indicative character. Painted scenes in the Italian style were rare, other than in the baroque sets of the masques performed at court. In the absence of visual realism, an effort was made to create spectacular effects with fight scenes, mime, simulated thunder, the use of firecrackers, and bags of bulls' blood to suggest bloodshed on stage. But it was above all the text and the actors' voices that generated the action and impressed it on the audience's imagination; thus Hamlet advised the actors who had come to Elsinore to speak their speeches "trippingly on the tongue" (*Hamlet*, III, ii).

The plays were performed in the county towns of England and sometimes at sea, on board ship. There were also foreign tours; for example, English actors put on *The Merchant of Venice* in Germany in 1611.

Many theaters were destroyed by order of Parliament in 1642. Their rebuilders during the Restoration (1660) found inspiration in the stage techniques current in France, adopting, for instance, the proscenium arch, which made visual illusion possible. The other great innovation was that female roles began to be played by actresses. During this period Shakespeare's plays were adapted to suit contemporary taste by dramatists such as Sir William Davenant, John Dryden, and Nahum Tate.

In the 18th century the English stage was dominated by the actor David

Mr. Garrick as King Lear

Left: David Garrick.

Garrick (1717–79), who was also manager of the Drury Lane Theatre in London from 1747 to 1776. He worked hard to make Shakespeare a national institution, even if his adaptations sometimes departed considerably from the original.

The period was, indeed, marked by the rise of great actors, the first "stars" of the stage, who owed their success to the Shakespearean repertoire. The Irish actor Charles Macklin (1699–1797) distinguished himself in his rendering, in 1741, of the part of Shylock, the Jew in *The Merchant of Venice,* a part he played again in 1789 when he was ninety years old.

Charles Kemble (1775–1854) played many Shakespearean parts, but the most memorable was that of King John, which he performed at Covent Garden in 1823, launching the fashion for period dress and elaborate historical reconstructions. His brother John Philip (1757–1823) managed the theaters of Drury Lane and Covent Garden, while also distinguishing himself as an actor and producer of the great tragedies and the Roman plays.

But the greatest of all was, without a doubt, Edmund Kean (1787–1833), whose first successes were in Drury Lane as Shylock in 1814 and then as Richard III; he also played the leading parts in the four great tragedies: *Hamlet, Othello, King Lear,* and *Macbeth.*

The actor William Macready (1793–1873), who managed the Covent Garden Theatre and then the Drury Lane Theatre, also played most of the great tragic roles. His chief merit was that he abandoned recent adaptations that were then still the rule in favor of Shakespeare's original texts.

John Philip Kemble as Hamlet, 1783.

The Victorian age was marked principally by the taste for historical reconstruction and visual display in theatrical productions—a fashion initiated by Sir Henry Irving (1838–1905), manager of the Lyceum Theatre from 1878 to 1902, and Sir Herbert Beerbohm Tree (1853–1917), manager of the Haymarket Theatre from 1887 to 1897.

In reaction to this emphasis on the spectacular, which tended to make performances distinctly heavy, William Poel (1852–1934) sought to re-create the conditions under which the Elizabethan stage had operated. He put on a shortened version of

Hamlet, taken from the first quarto edition, without scenery or interval. He had a profound influence on actors such as Harley Granville-Barker (1877–1946), who became famous for his productions of comedies, for example, *The Winter's Tale, Twelfth Night,* and *A Midsummer Night's Dream,* which he staged between 1912 and 1914. This marked the beginning of a great theatrical revival that spread rapidly throughout Europe.

The 20th century was responsible for a number of innovations. For example, Sir Barry Jackson (1879–1961) in 1925 staged *Hamlet* in modern dress, one way of asserting the reality of Shakespeare in contemporary life. Sir Tyrone Guthrie (1900–1971) successfully repeated this experiment in his 1953 production of *All's Well That Ends Well,* a play relatively rarely performed until then, which he helped to rediscover.

Such modernism made it possible to transpose the plays into a new context—an idea that underlay the success, hailed as one of the most

S ir Johnston Forbes-Robertson as Hamlet, 1902.

remarkable in the theater, of *A Midsummer Night's Dream* staged by Peter Brook (b. 1925) at Stratford in 1970. In this production he used the world of the circus as the modern equivalent of the magic and fairyland of the Athenian forest in which the young lovers take refuge. The cosmopolitan, multiracial, and multicultural character of Peter Brook's company adds to the originality of his productions. The accents and intonations of actors of British, African, Japanese, and Indian origin give a different and often unexpected resonance to Shakespeare's lines.

In an altogether different spirit, French director Ariane Mnouchkine found inspiration in the traditions of Japanese theater (Kabuki and No) in her 1981 production of *Richard II* at the Théâtre du Soleil in Vincennes. This play marked an epoch and influenced many productions all over the world.

In the mid-1970s the British producer Terry Hands, a member of the Royal Shakespeare Company, went to work at the Comédie Française in Paris to stage a number of Shakespeare's plays, notably *The Merchant of Venice* and a memorable *Twelfth Night.* In Italy the productions of Giorgio Strehler at the Piccolo Teatro in Milan (*King Lear, The Tempest*) are also recognized as brilliant and models of their kind.

Great Actors

They are too numerous for all to be named. But here are some of the most outstanding.

In England the Shakespearean repertoire remains an obligatory rite of passage in the career of every great actor or actress. Considering *Hamlet* alone, the best known and arguably the greatest of Shakespeare's plays, the list of the great renderings of the part of the melancholy prince of Denmark is long indeed.

In the Romantic period the great actors were John Philip Kemble, Edmund Kean, and William Macready, whom Sir Henry Irving succeeded at the Lyceum in 1874, when the fashion was for lavish productions. Sir Johnston Forbes-Robertson (1853–1937) played the title role in an 1897 production and went on to act it in a silent movie of 1913. Hamlet was also played by a woman, Sarah Bernhardt, in 1899. Sir Frank Robert Benson (1858–1939) was the first to put on the play in its complete original text at the Lyceum in 1899. In the United States in 1922 John Barrymore played the part more than a hundred times to spellbound audiences. Barry Jackson's Hamlet in modern dress in 1925 was a landmark, though the rendering by John Gielgud at the Old Vic in London in 1930, in which Hamlet was portrayed as the representative of a disillusioned generation, is still regarded by many critics as the best of the century. It was in 1937, in Tyrone Guthrie's production, that Laurence Olivier (1907–1991) played the part, to which he returned on screen ten years later. Alec Guinness also did a memorable rendering in a production at the Old Vic in 1938.

After the war the part was interpreted by Paul Scofield in 1948, Michael Redgrave at the Old Vic in 1950, then at Stratford eight years later. Peter O'Toole played Hamlet, directed by Laurence Olivier, in 1963 for the

J ohn Gielgud as Hamlet, 1934.

opening of London's National Theatre, while another actor—who won fame on the screen but was trained by the Royal Shakespeare Company—Richard Burton, played the part in New York in 1964. Hamlet was then acted by David Warner at Stratford and in London in 1965–6 and by Alan Howard in 1970. Ben Kingsley played a neuropathic Hamlet in a production staged by Buzz Goodbody in modern dress at the little Stratford theatre, The Other Place. Then came the interpretations of Derek Jacobi: first in 1978, again in Jonathan Pryce and Michael Pennington's film

P eter Brook's epoch-making 1970 production of *A Midsummer Night's Dream* with the Royal Shakespeare Company.

A little later Henry Purcell wrote his semi-opera *The Fairy Queen,* a version of *A Midsummer Night's Dream* in which sung passages alternate with spoken text. In the 18th century it continued to be the comedies that found favor with adapters. In 1716 the English singer and songwriter Richard Leveridge used extracts from *A Midsummer Night's Dream,* calling them *Pyramus and Thisbe* after the burlesque play within a play performed by the artisans. In 1744 the Italian composer Francesco Maria Veracini transposed *As You Like*

L aurence Olivier as Henry V in 1944.

for British television in 1980, and yet again in Anton Lesser's film in 1982. Most recently the part was tackled by a young actor, Mark Rylance, who rendered Hamlet as a complete psychotic, dressed in striped pajamas, as if Denmark were to him a vast psychiatric hospital.

Shakespeare and the Opera

Shakespeare's plays have often been adapted for operas based on specific scenes or characters—one being Falstaff, whom Italian composer Giuseppe Verdi (1813–1901) made the subject of an opera in 1893.

In the 17th century it was the comedies that inspired musicians and librettists. Thus Matthew Locke and Pelham Humfrey staged *The Tempest* in 1674.

It, taking his title, *Rosalind,* from the main character. It is known, too, that Mozart, shortly before he died, dreamed of composing music for an opera based on *The Tempest.* Toward the end of the century adaptations of the tragedies were also produced, such as Benda and Swanenberg's *Romeo and Juliet* in 1776.

In the 19th century it was Shakespeare's great tragedies that chiefly inspired the world of opera. *Romeo and Juliet* was frequently an inspiration to Romantic composers, yielding two great operas, one by Vincenzo Bellini in 1830, the other by Charles Gounod in 1867. Gioacchino Rossini's *Othello,* composed in 1816, is still famous for its willow song. Verdi presented *Macbeth* in 1847 and revised it in 1865. In this opera the music evokes the inner world of the conscience (Macbeth's crime, the queen's sleepwalking), as much as the outward action of the witches, animal cries, and the choir of people suffering tyranny.

In 1887 Verdi composed his own version of *Othello,* in which the essence of the conflict was reduced by Arrigo Boito's masterly adaptation to a vehicle for musical expression. But perhaps the greatest of all Shakespearean operas is Verdi's *Falstaff* (1893), adapted by Boito from *The Merry Wives of Windsor,* with added touches (like the aria on "honor") taken from the Henry IV plays.

Verdi also contemplated writing an opera based on *King Lear* at the end of his life, but unfortunately the project was never started. Wagner attempted a Shakespearean theme only once; his early opera *Das Liebesverbot* ("The prohibition of love," 1836), was

A poster for Verdi's *Otello.*

based on *Measure for Measure.*

The 20th century brought a return to the comedies, with Bedrich Smetana's *Viola* (1924), based on *Twelfth Night,* and *A Midsummer Night's Dream,* composed by Benjamin Britten in 1960. In the latter opera the voices are used to express the opposition of the supernatural world of the forest to the world of humans. By including familiar popular tunes, Britten successfully preserved the humorous effects of the play.

François Laroque

Shakespeare on Film

From the early days of movie-making to the present day, Shakespeare has inspired directors as widely varying in interpretative styles as Georges Méliès, Orson Welles, Franco Zeffirelli, Akira Kurosawa, Peter Greenaway, and Kenneth Branagh.

The age of silent films was a prolific one. One can count, in the first three decades of the 20th century, no fewer than seventeen *Hamlet*s, ten *Julius Caesar*s, eight *Macbeth*s, ten *Merchant of Venice*s. Most of these films, despite the contributions of film directors such as Georges Méliès or David Lewelyn Wark Griffith, are truncated adaptations and little more than filmed theatrical performances. An exception is the *Hamlet* filmed by Sir Johnston Forbes-Robertson and Cecil Hepworth in 1913. There are a few successful German films from the 1920s, specifically Hans Neumann's ribald rendering of *A Midsummer Night's Dream* (1925).

The advent of the "talkies" allowed Hollywood to reign supreme, featuring Max Reinhardt and William Dieterle's *A Midsummer Night's Dream* (1935)—in which thoroughly kitsch effects (the dance of the fairies in lace and tutus) appear side by side with disturbing hallucinations—and also George Cukor's *Romeo and Juliet* (1936). After the war Marlon Brando distinguished himself in Joseph Mankiewicz's *Julius Caesar* (1953), playing the part of Mark Antony. However, the film of *Antony and Cleopatra* by the same director, starring Elizabeth Taylor as Cleopatra, is a pasteboard spectacular in glorious technicolor that is best forgotten.

The first major successes came from Britain with the films of Laurence Olivier: *Henry V,* filmed in 1944 during World War II, ringing with patriotism and plunging us back into the Globe Theatre, which was reconstructed for the opening and closing scenes; *Hamlet* (1948), radically cut, without Rosencrantz or Guildenstern, in which the prince is represented from the outset as a young man unable to make

A scene from Hans Neumann's 1925 production of *A Midsummer Night's Dream.*

up his mind. These films were followed by two others, *Richard III,* filmed in 1955, and *Othello* in 1965, with Olivier in the title role, made up as a superb Ethiopian with ebony skin.

Orson Welles followed in his footsteps with *Macbeth,* filmed in 1948, *Othello* in 1952, and *Chimes at Midnight* in 1965 (consisting of scenes from *Richard II, Henry IV, Part 1* and *Part 2, The Merry Wives of Windsor,* and *Henry V).* This is probably the most successful of the three films, showing a great affection for the character of Falstaff, with whom Welles strongly identified.

Two Italian directors, Renato Castellani and Franco Zeffirelli, filmed English actors in the actual locations of the plays—Verona for *Romeo and Juliet* (Castellani, 1954; Zeffirelli, 1968) and Padua for *The Taming of the Shrew* (Zeffirelli, 1967). The film of this play starring Elizabeth Taylor and Richard Burton was enormously successful, as was *Romeo and Juliet* made the following year. Zeffirelli's choice of very young actors for Romeo and Juliet enabled him to portray the romantic cult of adolescent love destroyed by the incomprehension of parents.

Screen adaptations of Shakespeare in the postwar period were marked by the forceful contributions of Russian and Japanese film directors. Grigori Kosintsev, first of all, with a superb *Hamlet* in 1964, followed by *King Lear* in 1970: two films that were acclaimed as masterpieces by critics. Equally gripping and uncontestably even more original are the films of the Japanese director Akira Kurosawa. The first, made in 1957, is called *The Throne of Blood*—a brilliantly constructed film that transposes *Macbeth* to the medieval Japan of the samurai. By comparison Roman Polanski's *Macbeth,* filmed in 1971, seems much less subtle, though it holds a certain fascination with its powerful imagery, mingling realism and fantastic effects. Kurosawa returned to Shakespeare in 1985 with *Ran,* which moves *King Lear* to the heart of clan warfare, and enacts the tragedy of the old king in a world of declining feudalism, with ferocious battle scenes organized like ballets in dazzling colors.

Recent films show that Shakespeare continues to inspire film directors, yielding adaptations that demonstrate originality and talent. British actor Kenneth Branagh, who played the part of Henry V in Stratford and London before starting his own theater group, the Renaissance Theatre Company, brought Shakespeare's play *Henry V* to the screen in 1990. He cast himself in the role of the young king, next to actors such as Derek Jacobi, playing the Chorus, and Judi Dench, as the Hostess. This film, which deliberately takes a different direction from Laurence Olivier's, seems equally well realized. It

has been highly successful in the United States, England, and France. In 1991 Franco Zeffirelli tried his hand at tragedy, filming *Hamlet* in various Scottish castles, with the Australian actor Mel Gibson in the role of the prince. The same year Peter Greenaway, the British director of *The Draughtsman's Contract,* directed an adaptation of *The Tempest* called *Prospero's Books,* a densely packed spectacle, visually very successful. Sir John Gielgud, with the experience of his eighty-three years, plays an excellent Prospero and also lends his voice, modulated by computer, to all the other characters in the plot. In this film Prospero is the supreme manipulator: The play he writes under our eyes (he is also Shakespeare) incarnates and exorcises all his phantoms.

François Laroque

John Gielgud in *Prospero's Books,* directed by Peter Greenaway, 1991.

A Shakespeare Filmography

ANTONY AND CLEOPATRA
Cleopatra, d. Henry Andréani, 1910 (Fr.)
Cleopatra, d. Joseph Mankiewicz, with Elizabeth Taylor and Richard Burton, 1972 (Amer.)

AS YOU LIKE IT
d. Paul Czinner, with Laurence Olivier, 1936 (Eng.)

HAMLET
d. Clément Maurice, with Sarah Bernhardt, 1900 (Fr.)
d. Georges Méliès, 1907 (Fr.)
d. E. Hay Plumb, 1913 (Eng.)
d. Olivier, 1948 (Eng.)
Ophelia, d. Claude Chabrol, 1962
d. Grigori Kosintsev, 1964 (Russ.)
d. Tony Richardson, 1969 (Eng.)
d. Franco Zeffirelli, 1991 (Ital.)

HENRY IV, PARTS I AND 2
Chimes at Midnight, d. Orson Welles, 1965 (Span./Swiss)

HENRY V
d. Olivier, with Olivier, 1944 (Eng.)
d. Kenneth Branagh, with Branagh, 1990 (Eng.)

JULIUS CAESAR
The Death of Julius Caesar, d. Méliès, 1907 (Fr.)
d. David Bradley, with Charlton Heston, 1950 (Amer.)
d. Mankiewicz, with Marlon Brando, 1953 (Amer.)
d. Stuart Burge, with Heston and John Gielgud, 1969 (Eng.)

KING LEAR
d. Grigori Kosintsev, 1970 (Russ.)
d. Peter Brook, with Paul Scofield, 1971 (Dan.)
Ran, d. Akira Kurosawa, 1985 (Jap.)

MACBETH
d. André Calmettes, 1910 (Fr.)

d. Orson Welles, 1948 (Amer.)
The Throne of Blood, d. Kurosawa, 1957 (Jap.)
d. George Schaefer, 1960 (Eng.)
d. Roman Polanski, 1971 (Eng.)

THE MERCHANT OF VENICE
Shylock, d. Henri Desfontaines, 1913 (Fr.)
d. Peter Paul Felner, 1923

THE MERRY WIVES OF WINDSOR
d. Georg Wildhagen, 1950 (Ger.)

A MIDSUMMER NIGHT'S DREAM
d. Max Reinhardt/William Dieterle, with James Cagney, 1935 (Amer.)
d. Peter Hall, 1969 (Eng.)

MUCH ADO ABOUT NOTHING
d. Branagh, with Branagh, 1993 (Eng.)

OTHELLO
d. Welles, with Welles, 1952 (Amer.)
d. Sergei Yutkevitch, 1955 (Russ.)
d. Stuart Burge, with Olivier, 1965 (Eng.)

RICHARD III
d. Olivier, 1955 (Eng.)

ROMEO AND JULIET
d. George Cukor, 1936 (Amer.)
The Lovers of Verona, d. André Cayatte/Jacques Prévert, 1949 (Fr.)
d. Renato Castellani, 1954 (Ital./Eng.)
d. Zeffirelli, 1968 (Ital./Eng.)

THE TAMING OF THE SHREW
d. Desfontaines, 1911 (Fr.)
d. Zeffirelli, with Burton and Taylor, 1967 (Ital.)

THE TEMPEST
d. Derek Jarman, 1980 (Eng.)
d. Paul Mazursky, 1982 (Eng.)
Prospero's Books, d. Peter Greenaway, 1991 (Eng.)

TWELFTH NIGHT
d. Yan Fried, 1955 (Russ.)

THE WINTER'S TALE
d. Frank Dunlop, 1966 (Eng.)

The Shakespeare Industry

Every year some five thousand works about Shakespeare are published. Indeed, since the end of the Second World War a virtual industry has developed, producing books, theses, and articles on the playwright. Originating in American universities, the wave has now spread throughout Europe.

The volume of writing about Shakespeare far exceeds that available on any other English or American writer. Despite the great range of bibliographies, concordances, syntheses, summaries, and abstracts, it is difficult to keep up to date. The proliferation of critical material is, indeed, enough to discourage any student or scholar from embarking on the study of Shakespeare. Yet the craze shows no sign of abating in English- and German-speaking countries, where Shakespeare studies continue their relentless advance. In France and other Latin countries, where the difficult language of the plays is an obstacle, the situation is different. But

The Royal Shakespeare Theatre, Stratford.

new translations and editions, combined with the success of recent adaptations for stage and film, are likely to stimulate the still somewhat tentative French interest in Shakespeare.

The activities of the universities are matched by those of the theaters and actors. In Stratford-upon-Avon there are three permanent theaters: the Royal Shakespeare Theatre (RST), originally built in 1879 thanks to the generosity of Charles Edward Flower, a rich brewer of the region, and rebuilt after a fire in 1933; the little theater known as The Other Place, formerly used for rehearsals, which opened to the public in 1974 and was recently rebuilt to meet present-day safety standards; and the Swan Theatre, a wooden structure copied from the private theaters of the 17th century and adjoining the Royal Shakespeare Theatre. It opened its doors in 1986. The season lasts virtually the whole year (beginning in April with the official celebration of Shakespeare's birthday and finishing at the end of January) and runs concurrently with the same company's season at the Barbican Theatre in London. In the course of it some fifteen plays are performed, the most successful of which are put on at the Barbican. In addition to these theaters there are the National Theater, founded just before Shakespeare's quadricentenary and for a long time managed by Sir Laurence Olivier, the Young Vic, the Aldwych, and the open-air theater in Regent's Park, all of which feature Shakespeare's plays prominently.

Besides the Royal Shakespeare Company (the troupe in residence at the Royal Shakespeare Theatre and the Barbican), several new companies have been established in recent years, despite the severe financial pressures affecting

Shakespeare's birthplace as it was in 1769, 1851, and as it is today (top to bottom).

the British performing arts after public subsidies were reduced under Margaret Thatcher. These include the English Shakespeare Company, managed by Michael Bogdanov, and the Renaissance Theatre, managed by Kenneth Branagh, both with noteworthy productions to their credit. The plan to build a new Globe Theatre next to Shakespeare's theater, the foundations of which have recently been discovered, should soon become reality now that all the legal and financial obstacles to its construction have been removed. This is largely thanks to the efforts of Sam Wanamaker, an American actor who has devoted a considerable amount of time and energy to realizing the project.

In the summer visitors come in large numbers from all over the world to see the plays billed in the three Stratford theaters and to visit the town of Shakespeare's birth. The Japanese are particularly interested in this shrine of western culture. It was in fact in Tokyo that the 1991 world congress on Shakespeare took place, bringing together nearly one thousand delegates.

Shakespeare studies in their current dynamic state depend on a number of institutions. First of all there are the large specialized libraries—those of the Shakespeare Centre and the Shakespeare Institute at Stratford-upon-Avon, the Folger Shakespeare Library in Washington, D.C., and the Huntington Library at San Marino, California. Research in the form of articles, reports, and bibliographies is published and circulated in various periodicals. The oldest of these is *Shakespeare Jahrbuch* ("Shakespeare annual"), founded in 1865 in Berlin;

The Swan Theatre, Stratford.

the most prestigious, *Shakespeare Survey,* is published in Cambridge, England; the principal American publications are the *Shakespeare Quarterly,* launched in New York in 1950 and assumed by the Folger Library in 1972, and *Shakespeare Studies,* founded in Cincinnati in 1965. In France the review *Cahiers Elisabéthains* ("Elizabethan notebooks"), founded in 1972 at the Université Paul-Valéry of Montpellier, publishes some French and foreign research on Shakespeare and the Elizabethan period in its twice-yearly issues.

Most countries have a society for Shakespeare studies. The oldest is the German Shakespeare Society, founded in Weimar in 1865. The more recent French Shakespeare Society dates from 1975. One of the most active societies outside the United States, where there are a great many Shakespeareans, is the Shakespeare Society of Japan, now numbering eight hundred members—clear evidence of the popularity of the playwright's work in the Land of the Rising Sun. All these national societies belong to the International Shakespeare Association, founded in 1972, which organizes a world congress every four years. The first was held in Vancouver, British Columbia. But Stratford remains the mecca for Shakespeare studies, and it is there that the weeklong Shakespeare Conference is held in August every two years, bringing together at the Shakespeare Institute all the experts in the work of the great Elizabethan playwright.

François Laroque

Further Reading

Bentley, Gerald E., *The Professions of Dramatist and Player in Shakespeare's Time,* Princeton University Press, New Jersey, 1986

———, *Shakespeare: A Biographical Handbook,* Greenwood, Westport, Connecticut, 1986

Bradbrook, Muriel, *Artist and Society in Shakespeare's England,* Barnes and Noble Imports, Savage, Maryland, 1982

———, *Shakespeare: The Poet in His World,* Columbia University Press, New York, 1978

Bradley, Andew Cecil, *Shakespearean Tragedy,* Viking Penguin, New York, 1991

Brinkworth, E. R., *Shakespeare and the Bawdy Court of Stratford,* Rowman and Littlefield, Lanham, Maryland, 1972

Brooks, Harold F., Harold Jenkins, and Brian Morris, eds., *The Arden Shakespeare,* Routledge Chapman and Hall, New York, 1951

Bullough, Geoffrey, ed., *Narrative and Dramatic Sources of Shakespeare* (7 vols.), Columbia University Press, New York, 1957–

Chambers, Edmund K., *William Shakespeare: A Study of Facts and Problems,* Oxford University Press, New York, 1989

Coleridge, Samuel Taylor, *Shakespearean Criticism,* Biblio Distribution, Lanham, Maryland, 1980

Empson, William, *Essays on Shakespeare,* Cambridge University Press, New York, 1986

French, Marilyn, *Shakespeare's Division of Experience,* Ballantine, New York, 1983

Frye, Northrop, *On Shakespeare,* Yale University Press, New Haven, Connecticut, 1986

Granville-Barker, Harley, and George B. Harrison, *Companion to Shakespeare Studies,* Cambridge University Press, New York, 1934

Halliday, F. E., *Shakespeare,* Thames and Hudson, New York, 1986

Kott, Jan, *Shakespeare Our Contemporary,* W. W. Norton, New York, 1974

Laroque, François, *Shakespeare's Festive World: Elizabethan Seasonal Entertainment and the Professional Stage,* Cambridge University Press, New York, 1991

Lenz, Carolyn Ruth Swift, Gayle Greene, and Carol Thomas Neely, *The Woman's Part,* University of Illinois Press, Champaign, 1983

Levi, Peter, *The Life and Time of William Shakespeare,* Henry Holt and Co., New York, 1989

Muir, Kenneth, ed., *Interpretations of Shakespeare,* Oxford University Press, New York, 1987

———, *Shakespeare, the Comedies: A Collection of Critical Essays,* Prentice-Hall, Englewood Cliffs, New Jersey, 1985

Muir, Kenneth, et al., eds., *Shakespeare: Man of the Theater,* University of Delaware Press, Cranbury, New Jersey, 1983

Rowse, A. L., *Annotated Shakespeare,* Crown, New York, 1988

———, *Shakespeare the Man,* St. Martin's Press, New York, 1989

Rowse, A. L., ed., *The Contemporary Shakespeare Series* (7 vols.), University Press of America, Lanham, Maryland, 1984–

Schoenbaum, Samuel, *Shakespeare and the World,* Oxford University Press, New York, 1979

———, *Shakespeare's Lives,* Oxford University Press, New York, 1970

———, *William Shakespeare: A Documentary Life,* Oxford University Press, New York, 1975

Schücking, Levin L., *Character Problems in Shakespeare's Plays,* Peter Smith, Magnolia, Massachusetts, 1959

Spurgeon, Caroline, *Shakespeare's Imagery,* Cambridge University Press, New York, 1935

Taylor, Gary, *Reinventing Shakespeare,* Oxford University Press, New York, 1991

Tillyard, Eustace M., *The Elizabethan World Picture,* Random House, New York, 1959

Vickers, Brian, *Shakespeare: The Critical Heritage* (6 vols.), Routledge Chapman and Hall, New York, 1974

Wells, Stanley, *Shakespeare and the Elizabethans,* Cambridge University Press, New York, 1990

———, *Shakespeare in the Twentieth Century,* Cambridge University Press, New York, 1984

Wells, Stanley, ed., *The Cambridge Companion to Shakespeare Studies,* Cambridge University Press, New York, 1986

Chronology

1564 (26 April) Baptism of William, third child of John Shakespeare of Snitterfield and Mary Arden of Wilmcote

1568 John Shakespeare becomes bailiff of Stratford. The Queen's Men puts on plays in the town

1582 (28 November) William Shakespeare marries Anne Hathaway (born 1556)

1583 (26 May) Baptism of first daughter, Susanna

1585 (2 February) Baptism of twins, Hamnet and Judith

1587 The Queen's Men performs in Stratford. Shakespeare may have returned to London with the company

1588 The destruction of the Spanish Armada

1590–2 First performances of the historical trilogy *Henry VI*

1592 Philip Henslowe mentions a performance of *Henry VI* in his diary. The plague ravages London. Theaters are closed until 1594

1596 (11 August) Shakespeare's only son, Hamnet, dies

1597 Shakespeare buys New Place, his Stratford home

1598 The first publication of a play under Shakespeare's name—the quarto of *Love's Labour's Lost*

1598–9 The theater in Shoreditch is dismantled by James Burbage and rebuilt as the Globe at Southwark

1601 Performance of *Richard II* at the Globe

1603 Queen Elizabeth I dies. The Chamberlain's Men becomes the King's Men. In London thirty thousand die of the plague. King James I's arrival in the city is postponed by a year

1604–5 Gunpowder Plot to blow up the Houses of Parliament led by Guy Fawkes

1607 (5 June) Shakespeare's daughter Susanna marries John Hall, a well-known doctor in Stratford

1608 Shakespeare is one of the founders of Blackfriars Theatre

1610 Presumed year of Shakespeare's return to Stratford

1612 Shakespeare testifies in the Belott-Mountjoy suit. The earliest surviving example of his signature is at the end of his deposition

1613 (29 June) The Globe burns down

1616 (10 February) Shakespeare's daughter Judith marries Thomas Quiney. (25 March) Shakespeare signs his will. (23 April) Shakespeare dies and is buried two days later

1623 Death of Shakespeare's widow, Anne. First Folio published by Robert Heminge and Henry Condell

Shakespeare's Works

Plays

1590–1 *Henry VI, Part 2; Henry VI, Part 3*

1591–2 *Henry VI, Part 1*

1592–3 *Richard III; The Comedy of Errors*

1593–4 *Titus Andronicus; The Taming of the Shrew*

1594–5 *The Two Gentlemen of Verona; Love's Labour's Lost*

1595–6 *Romeo and Juliet; Richard II; A Midsummer Night's Dream*

1596–7 *King John; The Merchant of Venice*

1597–8 *Henry IV, Part 1; Henry IV, Part 2*

1598–9 *Much Ado About Nothing; Henry V; The Merry Wives of Windsor*

1599–1600 *Julius Caesar; As You Like It; Twelfth Night*

1600–1 *Hamlet*

1601–2 *Troilus and Cressida*

1602–3 *All's Well That Ends Well*

1604–5 *Measure for Measure; Othello*

1605–6 *Macbeth; King Lear*

1606–7 *Antony and Cleopatra; Timon of Athens*

1607–8 *Coriolanus*

1608–9 *Pericles*

1609–10 *Cymbeline*

1610–11 *The Winter's Tale*

1611–2 *The Tempest*

1612–3 *Henry VIII; The Two Noble Kinsmen*

Poems

1593 *Venus and Adonis*

1594 *The Rape of Lucrece*

1609 *The Sonnets*

List of Illustrations

Abbreviations: a=above; b=below; c=center; l=left; r=right; BL=British Library, London; BM=Department of Prints and Drawings, British Museum, London; Bodleian=Bodleian Library, Oxford; NPG=National Portrait Gallery, London; V&A=Victoria and Albert Museum, London

Front cover The "Flower" portrait of Shakespeare. Royal Shakespeare Theatre Collection, Stratford; and Cornelis Visscher. View of the City of London. Engraving, 1616. BM
Spine A writer or scholar, in an anonymous *Album Amicorum*, c. 1616. BL
Back cover Martin Droeshout. Portrait of William Shakespeare. Engraving on the title page of the First Folio, 1623. Bodleian
1 James I of England, in an anonymous *Album*

Amicorum, c.1616. BL
2–3 "On the Hill," in Michael van Meer, *Album Amicorum*, 1614–30. Edinburgh University Library
4–5 The Tower of London. *Ibid.*
6–7 Windsor Castle. *Ibid.*
8–9 A London scene. *Ibid.*
11 The "Chandos" portrait of Shakespeare. Anonymous painting, early 17th century. NPG
12 David Vinckboons. Traveling players at a village fair. Painting
13 Engraving in Hieronymus Bock, *De Stirpium, Maxime Earum Quae in Germania Nostra Nascuntur*, 1552
14 Map of England by Christopher Saxton, 1579. Royal Geographical Society, London
15 Engraving of a glover in Hartmann Schopper, *Panoplia, Omnium Illiberalium, Mechanicarum aut Sedentariarum Artium*, 1568

16–7a Record of William Shakespeare's baptism. Stratford church register. Shakespeare Birthplace Trust, Stratford
16–7c An Elizabethan school. Engraving
17br Title page of *A Short Introduction of Grammar*, 1607
18–9a Illustrations in an Elizabethan herbal. Bodleian
18–9c Embroidery, late 16th century. V&A
18–9b Engravings in George Turberville, *The Noble Art of Venerie*, 1575
20 Idem
21a Tapestry from Oxburgh, in Norfolk, England, 16th century. V&A
21c and 21b Engravings in Edward Topsell, *The History of the Serpents*, 1608, and *History of Four-Footed Beasts*, 1607
22 Engraving in Guy Marchant, *Kalendar and Compost of Shepherds*, 1493
23a A procession with Queen Elizabeth. BL

23b Woman carrying geese, in an anonymous *Album Amicorum*, c. 1616. BL
24–5a The Thames at Richmond. Flemish school. Fitzwilliam Museum, Cambridge
24–5c Musicians. Engravings in Thoinot Arbeau, *L'Orchesographie Traité en Forme de Dialogue*, 1538
24–5b Celebrations at the seat of the earl of Hertford. Engraving in John Nichols, *Progress and Entertainments of Queen Elizabeth*
26 Thomas Fisher. Copy of a scene from the Last Judgment in the Guild Chapel, Stratford. Watercolor, 1807. Art Collection of the Folger Shakespeare Library, Washington, D.C.
27a Hobbyhorse
27b Maypole dance in the time of Charles I. Bodleian
28a and 29a Tavern scenes of a meal and cardplayers. Watercolors,

Index

Acknowledgments

The author would like to thank Suzanne Bosman in London; Susan Brock; Stanley Wells, Director of the Shakespeare Institute in Birmingham; Christian Biet; Bernard Tannier; and the Centre d'Etudes et de Recherches Elisabéthaines of the Université Paul-Valéry at Montpellier, France

Photograph Credits

All rights reserved 12, 13, 15, 17br, 18–9b, 20, 21b, 21c, 22, 24–5b, 24–5c, 36–7, 37al, 37br, 38br, 38l, 39ar, 39l, 44–5b, 48b, 49, 52a, 54b, 56a, 57a, 59a, 63ar, 64–5b, 65a, 70, 71a, 84b, 88, 89a, 98–9b, 100a, 101b, 103a, 103br, 104a, 104b, 106–7a, 107b, 114b, 116–7b, 119al, 119ar, 129, 170, 180–1. Ashmolean Museum, Oxford 73al, 107ar. Marquess of Bath 56–7b. Bibliothek der Rijksuniversiteit, Utrecht 62a, 68. Bodleian Library, Oxford 27b, 76a, 84a, 108, back cover. Bridgeman Art Library 14, 18–9c, 21a, 40, 44–5a, 90, 91, 92–3, 101a, 109, 110–1a, 126, 151. British Film Institute, London 174b, 177. British Library, London 1, 23a, 23b, 29b, 37ar, 42–3b, 43a, 52–3b, 75ar, 76b, 82, 85ar, 85b, 89b, 105, 110–1b, 116–7a, 120, 143, 144, 145, spine. British Museum, London 46a, 46–7b, 60, 113a, front cover. Duke of Buccleuch and Queensberry KT 58a. Cahiers du Cinéma 178. Trustees of the Chatsworth Settlement 115l, 115r. Christie's Colour Library, London 34–5b. College of Arms, London 58–9b. Donald Cooper 174a. Corpus Christi College, Cambridge 50. Viscount De L'Isle MBE, Penshurst Place, Kent 98–9a. Dulwich College 55b, 69b. Dulwich Picture Gallery 73ac, 73ar, 83a. Edinburgh University Library 2–3, 4–5, 6–7, 8–9, 47a, 54–5a, 66–7, 110c, 112–3b. E.T. Archive 18–9a, 64a, 72a, 74–5, 92al, 93ar, 120–1, 122–3, 124–5. Fitzwilliam Museum, Cambridge 24–5a. Folger Shakespeare Library, Washington, D.C. 26, 28a, 29a, 57c, 87ar. Fotomas 16–7c, 34–5a, 94br. A. Fulgoni 139. Greater London Record Office 62bl. Guildhall Library, London 132. Louisa Hare 48a, 52b, 53a, 71b, 83b, 85al, 112a, 118a, 118b, 119cr. Ipswich Museums and Galleries 77, 78, 79, 80, 81a, 81b. Lefevre Gallery, London 169. Museum of London 69a. National Gallery, London 102–3a. National Portrait Gallery, London 11, 32–3, 51, 94ar, 94bl, 95, 102–3a, 114a, 116al. Private collections 54a, 102b, 116al. Public Record Office, London 126–7. Royal Armouries, London 99c. Royal Collection, courtesy of Her Majesty the Queen 96–7, 106. Royal Shakespeare Company 180–1, 183. Royal Shakespeare Theatre Collection, Stratford-upon-Avon 86, front cover. Scala 94al. Shakespeare Birthplace Trust, Stratford-upon-Avon 16–7a, 87al, 87b, 149, 170, 171, 172. Shakespeare Institute, University of Birmingham, England 61. Edwin Smith 182b. Society of Antiquaries, London 41. Stiftsarchiv, Rein, Austria 72–3b. Tate Gallery, London 165. Eileen Tweedy 158

Text Credits

Grateful acknowledgment is made for permission to use material from the following works: *Reinventing Shakespeare* by Gary Taylor, © 1989 by Gary Taylor (pp. 165–6); *Shakespeare's Division of Experience* by Marilyn French, © 1981, Marilyn French (pp. 168–9); *Shakespeare Our Contemporary* by Jan Kott, © 1964, Pánstwowe Wydawnictwo Naukowe (PWN Polish Scientific Publishers), Warszawa (pp. 166–7); *The Woman's Part* by Carolyn Ruth Swift Lenz, Gayle Greene, and Carol Thomas Neely, Copyright © 1980 by Carolyn Ruth Swift Lenz, Gayle Greene, and Carol Thomas Neely (p. 168)

François Laroque teaches English literature at the
Sorbonne in Paris. He is a Shakespeare specialist and
a member of the center for Elizabethan research
at Paul Valéry University in Montpellier, France.
In addition to numerous articles on Shakespeare's plays
and on the attitudes and folklore of Elizabethan England,
Laroque is also the author of *Shakespeare's Festive World:
Elizabethan Seasonal Entertainment and the Professional
Stage* (1991) and a collaborator on an anthology of
English literature (1991).

Translated from the French by Alexandra Campbell

Project Manager: Sharon AvRutick
Typographic Designer: Elissa Ichiyasu
Assistant Editor: Jennifer Stockman
Design Assistant: Penelope Hardy

Library of Congress Catalog Card Number: 93–70489

ISBN 0–8109–2890–6

Copyright © 1991 Gallimard

English translation copyright © 1993 Harry N. Abrams, Inc., New York,
and Thames and Hudson Ltd., London

Published in 1993 by Harry N. Abrams, Incorporated, New York
A Times Mirror Company

Printed and bound in Italy by Editoriale Libraria, Trieste